VOGUE
THICK KNITS

Christina Probert

Prentice Hall Press · New York

Acknowledgements

Colour photographs by Anthony Crickmay, 9, 11, 14, 15, 19, 24, 25, 27, 31, 33,34, 38, 41, 47, 52, 56, 57, 58, 60; Perry Ogden 4, 17, 20, 37, 44, 49, 54, 63; Mario Testino 6.

Black and white photographs by Duffy 26, 55; Hispard 61; Honeyman 23; McCabe 18; Ogden 4, 7, 8; Schiavone 17; Vernier 21.

Details by Dudley Mountney.

Hair by Nicky Clarke and Ashley Russell both of John Frieda 17; Anthony De May for Glemby 6; Pat Lewis for Vidal Sassoon 24, 25, 31, 33; Pascal 9, 11, 19; Trevor at Colombe 14, 15, 27; Kerry Warn of New York 4, 20.

Make-up by Arianne 14, 15, 27; Leslie Chilkes 6; Fran Cooper of New York 4, 20; Teresa Fairminer 24, 25, 31, 33; Mark Hayles 17; Pascal 9, 11, 19.

Clothes and accessories by Armani, Laura Ashley, Sheridan Barnett, Basile, Benetton, British Shoe Corporation, Brooks Brothers, Browns, Butler & Wilson, Comme des Garcons, Lawrence Corner, Paul Costello, Courtney, Crolla, Dickens & Jones, Perry Ellis, Fenn Wright & Manson, Fenwicks, Flip, Margaret Howell, Herbert Johnson, Katharine Hamnett, Harrods, Hennes, Herbert Johnson, Hobbs, Joseph, Kenzo, Kir, Calvin Klein, Lana Lino, Liberty, New & Lingwood, Mary Quant, John Marks, Maxmara, Mulberry, Options at Austin Reed, Benny Ong, Maxfield Parish, N. Peal, Andre Peters, Pollen, Marco Polo, Ralph Lauren, Russell & Bromley, The Scotch House, Sacha, Sunarma, Paul Smith, Tessiers, Tatters, Charles de Temple, Patricia Underwood, Whistles, The White House, Walkers, Zoran. International Textile Care Labelling Code courtesy of the Home Laundering Consultative Council.

Published by Prentice Hall Press
A division of Simon & Schuster, Inc.
Gulf + Western Building
One Gulf + Western Plaza
New York, N.Y. 10023

Originally published by Angell Editions, Newton Abbot, Devon

PRENTICE HALL PRESS is a trademark of Simon & Schuster, Inc.

Library of Congress Cataloging-in-Publication Data
Probert, Christina,
  Vogue thick knits.

  (Vogue knitting series)
  1. Knitting – Patterns. 2. Vogue (New York)
I. Title. II. Series.
TT820.P849 1986   746.9'2   86-9429

ISBN 0-13-943077-6

Printed in The Netherlands

10 9 8 7 6 5 4 3 2 1

First Prentice Hall Press Edition

Contents

Cowl-necked Seaman's Sweater

Comfortable, unisex, long and roomy stocking-stitch sweater in Aran yarn, with huge cowl neck, deep cuffs and hem welt in double rib

★ Suitable for beginners

MATERIALS

Yarn
Sunbeam Aran or Bainin
17(18:19) × 50g. balls

Needles
1 pair 5mm.
1 set of 4 double-pointed 4½mm.

MEASUREMENTS

Bust/Chest
Small (Medium : Large)
Length
69(71:72) cm.
27(27¾:28¼) in.

Sleeve Seam (including cuff)
58 cm.
22¾ in.

TENSION

9 sts. and 12 rows = 5 cm. (2 in.) square over st.st. on 5mm. needles. If your tension square does not correspond to these measurements, adjust the needle size used.

ABBREVIATIONS

k.=knit; p.=purl; st(s).=stitch(es); inc.= increase; dec.=decrease; beg.=begin(ning); rem. = remain(ing); rep. = repeat; alt. = alternate; tog. = together; sl. = slip stitch (transfer one stitch from left needle, knitwise unless otherwise stated, to right hand needle.); cont. = continue; patt. = pattern; foll. = following; folls. = follows; mm. = millimetres; cm. = centimetres; in. = inch(es); st.st. = stocking stitch; m.1 = make 1 st.: pick up horizontal loop lying before next st. and k. into the back of it.

BACK

** Cast on 86(90:94) sts. with 5mm. needles.
1st row: sl.1, k.1, * p.2, k.2, rep. from * to end.
2nd row: sl.1, k.3, p.2, * k.2, p.2, rep. from * to last 4 sts., k.4.

Rep. 1st and 2nd rows for 9 cm. (3½ in.), ending with a 2nd row.
Next row: sl.1, k. to end.
Foll row: sl.1, k.1, p. to last 2 sts., k.2. **
Rep. last 2 rows until back measures 69(71:72) cm. (27(27¾:28¼) in.) from beg., ending with a wrong side row.
Next row: cast off 26(28:30) sts. knitwise for shoulder, k.34 sts., including st. on needle, and sl. onto st. holder for collar, cast off 26(28:30) rem. sts. for 2nd shoulder.

FRONT

Work as for back from ** to **.
Cont. until front is 10 rows less than back to shoulders.

Shape Neck

Next row: k.35(37:39) sts., turn, leaving rem. sts. on spare needle, to be worked later.
Dec. 1 st. at neck edge on the next 9 rows.
Cast off 26(28:30) rem. sts. knitwise.
Leave centre 16 sts. on a st. holder, rejoin yarn to rem. sts. and complete to match 1st side.

SLEEVES

Cast on 66(66:70) sts. with 5mm. needles.
1st row: sl.1, k.1, * p.2, k.2, rep. from * to end.
2nd row: sl.1, k.3, p.2, * k.2, p.2, rep. from * to the last 4 sts., k.4.
Rep. 1st and 2nd rows for 13 cm. (5 in.), ending with a 2nd row.
Next row: sl.1, k. to end.
Foll. row: sl.1, k.1, p. to last 2 sts., k.2.
Rep. 1st and 2nd rows twice more.
Next row: k.2, m.1, k. to last 2 sts., m.1, k.2.
Cont. to inc. in this way at each end of every 6th row until there are 78(78:82) sts.
Work straight until sleeve measures 58 cm. (22¾ in.) from beg., ending with a wrong side row.
Cast off knitwise.

MAKING UP AND COLLAR

Press each piece lightly with warm iron and damp cloth.
Sew up shoulder seams.

Collar
With set of 4½mm. needles, pick up and k.18 sts. down left side of front neck edge, (k.1, p.1) into each st. on front st. holder, pick up and k.18 sts. up right side of neck, and (k.1, p.1) into each st. on back st. holder.
Work 15 cm. (5¾ in.) in rounds of k.2, p.2, rib.
Cast off in rib.
Sew up side seams, leaving 22 cm. (8½ in.) open for armholes.
Sew up sleeve seams, set in sleeves.
Press seams lightly.

Long, Crew-necked Sweater

Fisherman's rib sweater with ribbed welts, doubled-over collar and dropped shoulder line

★★ Suitable for knitters with some previous experience

MATERIALS

Yarn
Patons Clansman 4 ply
11(12:12:13) × 50g. balls

Needles
1 pair 2¾mm.
1 pair 3¼mm.

MEASUREMENTS

Bust
87(92:97:102) cm.
34(36:38:40) in.

Length
63(64:65:66) cm.
24¾(25:25½:26) in.

Sleeve Seam
48(48:49:49) cm.
18¾(18¾:19¼:19¼) in.

TENSION

26 sts. and 52 rows = 10 cm. (4 in.) square over patt. on 3¼mm. needles. If your tension square does not correspond to these measurements, adjust the needle size used.

ABBREVIATIONS

k.=knit; p.=purl; st(s).=stitch(es); inc.=increas(ing); dec.=decreas(ing); beg.=begin(ning); rem. = remain(ing); rep. = repeat; alt. = alternate; tog. = together; sl. = slip (transfer one stitch from left needle, knitwise unless otherwise stated, to right hand needle.); cont. = continue; patt. = pattern; foll. = following; folls. = follows; mm. = millimetres; cm. = centimetres; in. = inches; st. st. = stocking st.: one row k., one row p.; g. st. = garter st.: every row k.; incs. = increases; decs. = decreases; k.1b. = k. one below: k. into next st. one row below, at the same time sl. off st. above; p.s.s.o. = pass the sl. st. over.

FRONT

** Cast on 131(137:143:149) sts. with 2¾mm. needles.
1st row: k.2, * p.1, k.1, rep. from * to last st., k.1.
2nd row: * k.1, p.1, rep. from * to last st., k.1.
Rep. 1st and 2nd rows for 9 cm. (3½ in.), ending with a 2nd row.
Change to 3¼mm. needles and patt.
1st row (right side): k.
2nd row: k.1, * p.1, k.1b., rep. from * to last 2 sts., p.1, k.1.
These 2 rows form patt.
Work until front measures 42(42:43:43) cm. (16½(16½:16¾:16¾) in.) from beg., ending with a wrong side row.
Mark each end of last row to indicate beg. of armholes.

Shape Armholes
1st row: k.3, sl.1, k.2 tog., p.s.s.o., k. to last 6 sts., k.3 tog., k.3.
2nd to 4th rows: work in patt.
Rep. last 4 rows 4(5:5:6) times more. [111(113:119:121) sts.] **
Cont. until armholes measure 15(16:16:17) cm. (5¾(6¼:6¼:6½) in.) from markers, ending with a right side row.

Shape Neck
Next row: patt. 45(46:48:49) sts., cast off 21(21:23:23) sts., patt. to end.
Cont. on last set of sts.
Work 1 row.
Dec. 1 st. at neck edge on next row and then on every alt. row until 33(34:36:37) sts. rem.
Work 6 rows, ending at armhole edge.

Shape Shoulder
Cast off 4(4:6:6) sts. at beg. of next row and 5(5:5:5) sts. at beg. of 5 foll. alt. rows.
Work 1 row.
Cast off 4(5:5:6) sts.
Rejoin yarn to rem. sts. at neck edge and work to match first side, working one row more to end at armhole edge before shaping shoulder.

BACK

Work as for front from ** to **.
Cont. until armholes measure same as front to shoulder shaping, ending with a wrong side row.

Shape Shoulder and Back Neck
Cast off 4(4:6:6) sts. at beg. of next 2 rows and 5(5:5:5) sts. at beg. of 4 foll. rows.
Next row: cast off 5(5:5:5) sts., k. 19(20:20:21) sts. including st. on needle, cast off 35(35:37:37) sts., k. to end.
Cont. on last set of sts.
1st row: cast off 5(5:5:5) sts., patt. to last 2 sts., k.2 tog.
2nd row: k.2 tog., k. to end.
Rep. 1st and 2nd rows once more and then 1st row again.
Work 1 row.
Cast off rem. 4(5:5:6) sts.
Rejoin yarn to rem. sts. at neck edge.
1st row: k.2 tog., patt. to end.
2nd row: cast off 5(5:5:5) sts., k. to last 2 sts., k.2 tog.
Rep. 1st and 2nd rows once more and then 1st row again.
Cast off rem. 4(5:5:6) sts.

SLEEVES

Cast on 61(65:65:69) sts. with 2¾mm. needles.
Work 8 cm. (3¼ in.) in rib as front, ending with a 2nd row.
Change to 3¼mm. needles and patt.
Work 4 rows.
Inc. 1 st. at each end of next and every 8th row until there are 109(113:113:117) sts., working inc. sts. into patt.
Work until sleeve measures 48(48:49:49) cm. (18¾(18¾:19¼:19¼) in.), ending with a wrong side row.

Shape Top

1st row: k.3, sl.1, k.2 tog., p.s.s.o., k. to last 6 sts., k.3 tog., k.3.
2nd to 4th rows: work in patt.
Rep. last 4 rows 4(5:5:6) times more.
Cast off.

MAKING UP

Press each piece lightly.
Sew up right shoulder seam.

Neck Border

With right side facing and 2¾mm. needles, k. up 31(31:31:31) sts. evenly down left side of front neck edge, 21(21:23:23) sts. from cast off sts., 30(30:30:30) sts. up right side of neck and 55(55:57:57) sts. evenly along back neck edge. [137(137:141:141) sts.]
1st to 4th rows: k.
5th row: * k.1, p.1, rep. from * to last st., k.1.

6th row: k.2, * p.1, k.1, rep. from * to last st., k.1.
Rep. 5th and 6th rows 8 more times.
Cast off loosely in rib.
Sew up left shoulder and neck border seam.
Fold ribbing of neck border in half onto wrong side and slip st. down.
Sew up side and sleeve seams.
Set in sleeves.
Press seams.

Simple Garter Stitch Jacket

Body-hugging, hip-length garter stitch jacket with four pockets, the lower body and sleeves worked sideways, edged with crochet

★★ Suitable for knitters with some previous experience

MATERIALS

Yarn
Patons Diploma Aran
13(14:15) × 50g. balls

Needles
1 pair 4mm.
1 4mm. crochet hook
Stitch holder

Buttons
5 (large)
2 (small)

MEASUREMENTS

Bust
82(87:92) cm
32(34:36) in.

Length (from top of shoulders)
53(54:54) cm.
20¾(21¼:21¼) in.

Sleeve Seam
51 cm.
20 in.

TENSION

9 sts. and 18 rows = 5 cm. (2 in.) square over garter stitch on 4mm. needles. If your tension square does not correspond to these measurements, adjust the needle size used.

ABBREVIATIONS

k.=knit; p.=purl; st(s).=stitch(es); inc.= increase; dec.=decrease; beg.=begin(ning);

rem. = remain(ing); rep. = repeat; alt. = alternate; tog. = together; sl. = slip stitch (transfer one stitch from left needle, knitwise unless otherwise stated, to right hand needle.); cont. = continue; patt. = pattern; foll. = following; folls. = follows; mm. = millimetres; cm. = centimetre(s); in. = inch(es); y.fwd. = yarn forward; y.r.n. = yarn round needle; d.c. = double crochet; ch. = chain; sp. = space; g.st. = garter stitch .

BACK AND FRONTS (worked sideways in one piece)

Cast on 68 sts. fairly loosely.
Work in g.st. for 19(20:21) cm. (7½(7¾:8¼) in.).
** **Shape Armhole**
Dec. 1 st. at beg. of next and foll. 3 alt. rows.
Work 5 rows straight.
Now inc. 1 st. at beg. of next and foll. 3 alt. rows. **
Work 38(41:43) cm. (15(16:16¾) in.) straight, then rep. from ** to **.
Work a further 19(20:21) cm. (7½(7¾:8¼) in.) straight.
Cast off knitwise.
With right side facing, pick up and k. 68(72:77) sts. across top edge of back for yoke, and work 15(17:17) cm. (5¾(6½:6½) in.) straight in g.st.
Next row: k.23(24:26), cast off 22(24:25) sts. for back neck, k. 23(24:26), including st. on needle after casting off.
Cont. on last group of 23(24:26) sts. for first side and work 8 rows straight.
Now shape front by inc. 1 st. at inside edge on next and every foll. 3rd row until there are 36(38:42) sts., taking inc. sts. into g.st.

Work straight until front measures 17(18:18) cm. (6½(7:7) in.) from neck casting off.

Make Pocket Flap
Next row: k.12(13:14), turn and leave rem. sts. on a spare needle.
Cont. on these 12(13:14) sts. and k. 1 row.
Cast off. Slip next 12(12:14) sts. onto a stitch holder. Rejoin yarn to rem. 12(13:14) sts. and k. 2 rows.
Cast off.
Rejoin yarn to 12(12:14) sts. on stitch holder and work as folls.:
1st row: k.2 tog., k. to last 2 sts., k.2 tog.
2nd row: k.4(4:5), (work y.fwd. and y.r.n.), k.2 tog., k.4(4:5).

3rd row: k.5(5:6), k.1, letting extra loop (formed by y.fwd. and y.r.n.) fall, k.4(4:5). Cont. in g.st., dec. 1 st. at each end of every row until 6 sts. rem.
Cast off.
Rejoin yarn to rem. 23(24:26) sts. and finish to correspond with first side.

SLEEVES

Cast on 90 sts., k.2 rows.

Shape Top
Inc. 1 st. at beg. of next and every foll. alt. row until there are 102(104:104) sts.
Work 1 row straight.
1st and 2nd rows: inc. in 1st st., k.20, turn and work back.
3rd and 4th rows: inc. in 1st st., k.26, turn and work back.
5th and 6th rows: inc. in 1st st., k.32, turn and work back.
Cont. inc. 1 st. at top of sleeve on next and every foll. alt. row and *at the same time* work 6 sts. more on next and every alt. row until the rows 'inc. in 1st st., k.74, turn and work back' have been worked.
Now keep top edge of sleeve straight and cont. 'working 6 sts. more on next and every alt. row as before until the rows 'k.104, turn and work back' have been worked.

Now work 6 sts. less on next and every alt. row until the rows 'k.74, turn and work back' have been worked.
Next 2 rows: k.2 tog., k.68, turn and work back.
Next 2 rows: k.2 tog., k.62, turn and work back.
Cont. dec. 1 st. at top edge of sleeve on next and every alt. row and *at the same time* cont. working 5 sts. less on next and every alt. row until the rows 'k.2 tog., k.20, turn and work back' have been worked.
Cont. dec. at top edge on next and every alt. row until 90 sts. rem.
Work 2 rows straight.
Cast off.

POCKET

Cast on 22 sts. and work 8 cm. (3¼ in.) in g.st.
Work buttonhole in next 2 rows as folls.:
1st buttonhole row: k.10, work y.fwd. and y.r.n., k.2 tog., k.10.
2nd buttonhole row: k. back, letting extra loop (formed by the y.fwd., and y.r.n.) fall from needle.
Work a further 2 rows in g.st. Cast off.
Make another pocket in the same manner.

LINING FOR TOP POCKET

Cast on 12(12:14) sts. and work 7 cm. (2¾ in.) in g.st. Cast off.

MAKING UP

Press work very lightly, taking care not to spoil g.st. patt.
Sew 2 pieces of yoke to fronts. Sew up sleeve and side seams.
Set in sleeves.
Pin a pocket in centre of each front, bottom of pocket to come 5 cm. (2 in.) above lower edge, sew in position.
Pin linings for the top pockets in position, then slipstitch neatly all round.
With right side facing, using 4mm. crochet hook, start at lower edge and work in d.c. up right front, all round neck and down left front.
Turn and work a further row in d.c.
Cont. in d.c., making 3 buttonholes on right front in next row, 1st to come at join of yoke and body, and 2nd and 3rd spaced at 13 cm. (5 in.) intervals, first marking position of buttons on left front with pins to ensure even spacing, then working holes as folls., to correspond:

1st buttonhole row: work to position of hole, make 4 ch., miss 3 d.c.
2nd buttonhole row: work back in d.c., working 3 d.c. into each 4 ch. space.
Work a further 2 rows in d.c. Fasten off.
Work a row of d.c. all round lower edge of jacket and round each pocket flap.
Press seams lightly. Sew on buttons.

Chunky Wool Double-breasted Coat

Double-breasted short coat with saddle sleeves, collar, pockets in side seams, knitted in stocking stitch with ribbed details

★ Suitable for beginners

MATERIALS

Yarn
Jaeger Naturgarn
16(17:18) × 100g. hanks

Needles
1 pair 5½mm.
1 6mm. crochet hook

Buttons
10 (large)
1 (small)

MEASUREMENTS

Bust
87(92:97) cm.
34(36:38) in.

Length (from top of shoulders)
102(104:104) cm.
40(41:41) in.

Sleeve Seam
36 cm.
14 in.

TENSION

16 sts. and 20 rows = 10 cm. (4 in.) square over stocking stitch on 5½mm. needles. If your tension square does not correspond to these measurements, adjust the needle size used.

ABBREVIATIONS

k.=knit; p.=purl; st(s).=stitch(es); inc.= increase; dec.=decrease; beg.=begin(ning); rem. = remain(ing); rep. = repeat; alt. =

LEFT FRONT

Cast on 66(68:70) sts.
1st row (right side): * k.1, p.1, rep. from * to end.
Rep. 1st row until work measures 18 cm. (7 in.) at centre from start, ending with right side facing.
Next row: k.37(39:41), rib to end.
Next row: rib 29, p.37(39:41).
Rep. last 2 rows until front side edge matches back to armhole, ending with right side facing.

Shape Armhole

Cast off 6 sts. at beg. of next row. Work 1 row straight, then dec. 1 st. at armhole edge on every row until 52(54:56) sts. rem. Now dec. 1 st. at beg. of next and every alt. row until 48(49:50) sts. rem.
Work straight until front matches back armhole edge, ending with wrong side facing.

Shape Neck and Shoulder

1st row: cast off 23(24:24) sts., work to end.
2nd row: cast off 7(7:6) sts., work to end.
3rd row: cast off 3 sts., work to end.
4th row: cast off 6(6:7) sts., work to end.
5th row: as 3rd.
Cast off rem. 6(6:7) sts.

RIGHT FRONT

Cast on 66(68:70) sts.
1st row (right side): * p.1, k.1, rep. from * to end.
Rep. 1st row until work measures 18 cm. (7 in.) at centre from start, ending with right side facing.
Next row: rib 29, k. to end.
Next row: p.37(39:41), rib to end.
Finish to correspond with left front, working 5 pairs of buttonholes, 1st pair to come 29 cm. (11¼ in.) from beg., 5th pair in 5th and 6th rows below neck shaping and rest spaced evenly between. Mark position of buttons on left front with pins, then work holes to correspond.
To make a pair of buttonholes (right side facing): rib 3, cast off 3, rib 17, cast off 3, work to end. Work back, casting on 3 sts. over those cast off.

RIGHT SLEEVE

** Cast on 51(53:55) sts. and, starting with 1st row, work 10 rows in k.1, p.1 rib as for back.
Cont.in rib, shaping sides by inc. 1 st. at each end of next and every foll. 8th row until there are 65(67:69) sts., taking inc. sts. into rib.
Work straight until sleeve seam measures 36 cm. (14 in.), ending with right side facing.

Shape Top

Cast off 6 sts. at beg. of next 2 rows, then dec. 1 st. at each end of next and every alt. row until 33(35:39) sts. rem.
Work 1 row straight, then dec. 1 st. at each end of every row until 15 sts. rem., all sizes.

Continue straight on these 15 sts. for saddle until strip fits along shoulder edge when slightly stretched, ** ending with right side facing (front edge).

Shape Top

Cast off 5 sts. at beg. of next and foll. 2 alt. rows.

LEFT SLEEVE

Work as for right sleeve from ** to ** but ending with wrong side facing (front edge).
Shape top as for right sleeve.

COLLAR

Cast on 85 sts. and work in k.1, p.1 rib as for back until work measures 14 cm. (5½ in.) at centre from start, ending with 1st row.

Shape Top

Next 2 rows: rib to last 12 sts., turn, sl.1.
Next 2 rows: rib to last 24 sts., turn, sl.1.
Next 2 rows: rib to last 36 sts., turn, sl.1.
Next 2 rows: rib all sts., picking up a loop at each point where work was turned and working it tog. with next st. to avoid a hole. Cast off very firmly in rib.

POCKET LININGS

Right: cast on 11 sts. and p.1 row. Cont. in st.st., inc. 1st. at beg. of every k. row until there are 25 sts.
Work straight until lining measures 14 cm. (5½ in.) at centre from start, ending with a p. row.
Now dec. 1 st. at beg. of next row, then at this edge on every row until 9 sts. rem. Cast off.
Left: work to correspond with right lining, working shapings at other end of row.

MAKING UP

Following instructions on the ball band, press work lightly on wrong side, omitting ribbing.
Join side seams leaving a 17 cm. (6½ in.) opening on each side for pockets, top of opening to come 18 cm. (7 in.) below armhole.
Pin lining in position, right side of lining to wrong side of work, longer straight edge towards back; sew in position all round. With crochet hook work slip stitch along front edge of pocket and short edges of collar. Join sleeve seams; insert sleeves, with saddle strips along shoulders on back and front, with longer edge towards back. Work slip stitch up right front edge, make 2 ch. for buttonloop at corner, then along 16(17:17) cast off sts. for neck, then cont. round neck edge to left corner, then work down left front edge.
Sew shaped edge of collar round neck, starting and ending at beg. of neck shaping. Press all seams. Sew on buttons, sewing small button on left front opposite buttonloop.

alternate; tog. = together; sl. = slip stitch (transfer one stitch from left needle, purlwise unless otherwise stated, to right hand needle.); cont. = continue; patt. = pattern; foll. = following; folls. = follows; mm. = millimetres; cm. = centimetre(s); in. = inch(es); p.s.s.o. = pass the slipped st. over; t.b.l. = through back of loops; st. st. = stocking stitch; ch. = chain.
NOTE: Coat will drop approx 4 cm. (1½ in.) in wear.

BACK

Cast on 95(99:103) sts.
1st row (right side): k.1, * p.1, k.1, rep. from * to end.
2nd row: p.1, * k.1, p.1, rep. from * to end.
Rep. last 2 rows until work measures 18 cm. (7 in.) at centre from start, ending with right side facing.
Change to st.st., starting with a k. row, and work straight until back measures 76(77:77) cm. (29¾:30¼:30¼ in.) at centre from start, ending with a p. row.

Shape Armholes

Cast off 6 sts. at beg. of next 2 rows.
Next row: k.2 tog., k. to last 2 sts., sl.1, k.1, p.s.s.o.
Next row: p.2 tog. t.b.l., p. to last 2 sts., p.2 tog.
Rep. last 2 rows 3 times more. [67(71:75) sts.]
Next row: k.2 tog., k. to last 2 sts., sl.1, k.1, p.s.s.o.
Next row: p.
Rep. last 2 rows until 59(61:63) sts. rem. Work straight until back measures 94(97:97) cm. (37(38:38) in.) at centre from beg., ending with a p. row.

Shape Shoulders

Cast off 7(7:6) sts. at beg. of next 2 rows, then 6(6:7) sts. at beg. of next 4 rows. Cast off rem. 21(23:23) sts.

Thick Check Pattern Coat

Thigh-length raised check pattern coat with doubled collar, hemmed cuffs and lower edge, button bands backed with binding tape

★★ Suitable for knitters with some previous experience

MATERIALS

Yarn
Emu Super Match DK (used double)
24(24:26) × 50g. balls

Needles
1 pair 4½mm.
1 pair 5½mm.

Buttons
5

Binding Tape
1.50 metres
1½ yards

MEASUREMENTS

Bust
82–87(87–92:92–97) cm.
32–34(34–36:36–38) in.

Length
74(74:76) cm.
29(29:29¾) in.

Sleeve Seam
41(41:43) cm.
16(16:16¾) in.

TENSION

7½ sts. and 10 rows = 5 cm. (2 in.) square over pattern on 5½mm. needles. If your tension square does not correspond to these measurements, adjust the needle size used.

ABBREVIATIONS

k.=knit; p.=purl; st(s).=stitch(es); inc.= increase; dec.=decrease; beg.=begin(ning); rem. = remain(ing); rep. = repeat; alt. = alternate; tog. = together; sl. = slip stitch (transfer one stitch from left needle, knitwise unless otherwise stated, to right hand needle.); cont. = continue; patt. = pattern; foll. = following; folls. = follows; mm. = millimetres; cm. = centimetre(s); in. = inch(es); y.bk. = yarn back; y.fwd. = yarn forward; st.st. = stocking stitch. NOTE: Yarn is used double throughout. When working sl.1 in pattern, the stitch should always be slipped purlwise, keeping the yarn at the front (right side) of the work.

BACK

Cast on 74(78:82) sts. using double yarn and 4½mm. needles. Work 9 rows in st. st., beg. with k. row.

10th row: k., to mark hemline. Change to 5½mm. needles and cont. in patt. thus:
1st row: k.6(8:10), p.2, *(sl.1, k.1, sl.1, k.1, p.2) twice, k.10, p.2, rep. from * to last 18(20:22); sts., (sl.1, k.1, sl.1, k.1, p.2) twice, k.6(8:10).
2nd and 4th rows: p.6(8:10), *(k.2, p.4) twice, k.2, p.10, rep. from * to last 20(22:24) sts., (k.2, p.4) twice, k.2, p.6(8:10).
3rd row: k.6(8:10), p.2, *(k.1, sl.1, k.1, sl.1, p.2) twice, k.10, p.2, rep. from * to last 18(20:22) sts., (k.1, sl.1, k.1, sl.1, p.2) twice, k.6(8:10).
Rep. 1st–4th rows inclusive twice more.
13th row: as 1st.
14th row: as 2nd.
15th row: p.
16th row: k.
17th row: (sl.1, k.1) 0(1:2) times, p.2, sl.1, k.1, sl.1, k.1, p.2, * k.10, p.2, (sl.1, k.1, sl.1, k.1, p.2) twice, rep. from * to last 18(20:22) sts., k.10, p.2, sl.1, k.1, sl.1, k.1, p.2, (sl.1, k.1) 0(1:2) times.
18th and 20th rows: p.0(2:4), k.2, p.4, *k.2, p.10. (k.2, p.4) twice, * rep. from * to *, but ending p.0(2:4).
19th row: (k.1, sl.1) 0(1:2) times, p.2, k.1, sl.1, k.1, sl.1, p.2, *k.10, p.2, (k.1, sl.1, k.1, sl.1, p.2) twice, rep. from * to last 18(20:22) sts., k.10, p.2, k.1, sl.1, k.1, sl.1, p.2, (k.1, sl.1) 0(1:2) times.
Rep. 17th–20th rows inclusive twice more.
29th row: as 17th.
30th row: as 18th.
31st row: p.
32nd row: k.
Cont. to rep. these 32 rows until work measures 53(53:54) cm. (20¾(20¾:21¼) in.) from beg. of patt.

Shape Armholes
Cast off 2 sts. at beg. of next 2 rows.
Dec. 1 st. at each end of every row until 60(62:66) sts. rem.
Cont. straight on these sts. until work measures 21(21:22) cm. (8¼(8¼:8½) in.) from beg. of armholes.

Shape Shoulders
Cast off 7 sts. at beg. of next 4 rows, then cast off 6(6:7) sts. at beg. of next 2 rows.
Cast off rem. 20(22:24) sts.

POCKET LINING

Cast on 22 sts. with 5½mm. needles.
Work 34 rows in st.st.
Leave sts. on stitch holder.

LEFT FRONT

Cast on 44(46:48) sts. with 4½mm. needles.

Work 9 rows in st.st.
10th row: k.
Change to 5½mm. needles, cont. in patt.:
1st row: k.6(8:10), p.2, (sl.1, k.1, sl.1, k.1, p.2) twice, k.10, p.2, (sl.1, k.1, sl.1, k.1, p.2) twice.
This row sets patt.
Cont. in patt. as for back until 48 rows have been worked.
49th row: patt. 2, sl. 22 sts. onto stitch holder, patt. 22 sts. of pocket lining, patt. to end.
Cont. until work corresponds with back to armholes, ending with a p. row.

Shape Armholes
Cast off 2 sts. at beg. of next row. Work 1 row.
Dec. 1 st. at armhole edge on every row until 37(38:40) sts. rem.
Cont. straight on these sts. until work measures 16(16:17) cm. (6¼(6¼:6½) in.) from beg. of the armholes, ending at

centre front edge. Cast off 6(8:9) sts. at beg. of next row, dec. 1 st. at neck edge every row until 20(20:21) sts. rem.
Cont. straight until work corresponds with back to shoulders, ending at arm-hole edge.
Cast off 7(8:9) sts. at beg. of next and foll. alt. row.
Cast off 6(6:7) rem. sts.
With 4½mm. needles and right side facing, slip pocket sts. left on holder onto needle and work 1 row k., 1 row p., for 8 rows.
Cast off these sts.
Slipstitch pocket edging on inside of pocket top. Sew facing in position.

RIGHT FRONT

Work pocket lining as before with 5½mm. needles.
Cast on 44(46:48) sts. with 4½mm. needles.
Work 9 rows in st.st.
10th row: k.
Change to 5½mm. needles.
1st row: p.2, (sl.1, k.1, sl.1, k.1, p.2) twice, k.10, p.2, (sl.1, k.1, sl.1, k.1, p.2) twice, k.6(8:10). This row sets patt.
Cont. in patt. and work buttonholes every 27th and 28th rows thus: work 3 sts., cast off 4 sts., work to end.
Next row: work along row and cast on 4 sts. above the sts. cast off in previous row.
Cont. to work in pattern as for left front, reversing all shaping instructions.

SLEEVES

Cast on 40(42:44) sts. with 4½mm. needles.
Work 9 rows in st.st.
10th row: k.
Change to 5½mm. needles.
1st row: k.1(2:3), p.2, (sl.1, k.1, sl.1, k.1, p.2) twice, k.10, p.2, (sl.1, k.1, sl.1, k.1, p.2) twice, k.1(2:3). This row sets patt. Cont. in patt. and inc. 1 st. at each end 9th and every foll. 8th row until there are 54(58:62) sts.
Cont. straight on these sts. until work measures 41(41:43) cm. (16(16:16¾) in.) from beg. of patt. or length required.

Shape Top

Cast off 2 sts. at beg. of next 2 rows. Dec. 1 st. at each end of next and every foll. 4th row until 40(42:44) sts. rem., then dec. 1 st. at each end of every alt. row until 28(30:32) sts. rem.
Dec. 1 st. at each end of every row until 16(18:18) sts. rem.
Cast off rem. sts.

COLLAR

Cast on 26 sts. with 4½mm. needles.
K.1 row, then cont. in st.st.
Cast on 5 sts. at beg. of next 8 rows.
Inc. 1 st. at each end of next 2 rows. [70 sts.]
Work 5 rows straight. Inc. 1 st. at each end of next and every foll. 5th row until 80 sts. rem.

Work 4 rows straight, ending with a k. row.

Next row: k. Change to 5½mm. needles.

1st row: k.9, * p.2, (leave yarn at front, sl.1, y.bk., k.1, y.fwd., sl.1, y.bk., k.1, p.2) twice, k.10, * rep. from * to *, but ending last rep. k.9. This row sets patt.

Dec. 1 st. at each end of every 5th row until 70 sts. rem.

Work 6 rows straight. Dec. 1 st. at each end of next 2 rows. Cast off 5 sts. at beg. of next 8 rows.

Cast off rem. sts.

MAKING UP

Press all pieces lightly on reverse side.

Sew in all ends. Backstitch shoulder, side and sleeve seams, turn up hem and cuffs and stitch.

With right sides together, stitch collar sides. Turn, then stitch collar into position.

Sew binding tape down each front, sew round buttonholes, sew on buttons.

Overchecked Husky Sweater

V-neck, unisex sweater with raglan sleeves and ribbed welts, in two-tone slipped-stitch overcheck pattern

★★ Suitable for knitters with some previous experience

MATERIALS

Yarn
Hayfield Grampian Chunky
11(11:12:13:13) × 50g. balls (Main Col. A)
5(6:6:7:7) × 50g. balls (Contrast Col. B)

Needles
1 pair 5½mm.
1 pair 6½mm.
1 set of 4 double-pointed 5½mm.
Stitch holder.

MEASUREMENTS

Chest
92(97:102:107:112) cm.
36(38:40:42:44) in.

Length
66(67:68:69:70) cm.
26(26¼:26¾:27:27½) in.

Sleeve Seam
46(47:48:49:50) cm.
18(18½:18¾:19¼:19½) in.

TENSION

14 sts. and 24 rows = 10 cm. (4 in.) square over patt. on 6½mm. needles. If your tension square does not correspond to these measurements, adjust the needle size used.

ABBREVIATIONS

k.=knit; p.=purl; st(s).=stitch(es); inc.= increase; dec.=decrease; beg.=begin(ning); rem. = remain(ing); rep. = repeat; alt. = alternate; tog. = together; sl. = slip stitch (transfer one stitch from left needle, knit-wise unless otherwise stated, to right hand needle.); cont. = continue; patt. = pattern; foll. = following; folls. = follows; mm. = millimetres; cm. = centimetres; in. = inch(es); st.st. = stocking stitch; sl.1P = slip stitch purlwise; p.s.s.o. = pass the sl. st. over.

BACK

Cast on 71(75:79:83:87) sts. with 5½mm. needles and A.

1st row: k.1, * p.1, k.1, rep. from * to end.

2nd row: p.1, * k.1, p,1, rep. from * to end.

Rep. these 2 rows for 9 cm. (3½ in.) ending with 2nd row. Change to 6½mm. needles and cont. in patt. as folls.:

1st row: with A, k. to end.

2nd row: with A, k.3, * p.1, k.3, rep. from * to end.

3rd row: with B, k.1, * sl.1P, k.1, rep. from * to end, keeping yarn at back of work when slipping sts.

4th row: with B, p.1, * sl.1P, p.1, rep. from * to end, keeping yarn at front (wrong side) of work when slipping sts.

These 4 rows form the patt. and are rep. throughout.

Cont. in patt. until work measures 43 cm. (16¾ in.) from beg., ending with 4th row.

Shape Raglan

Keeping patt. correct, cast off 3 sts. at beg. of next 2 rows, then work 2 rows.

Dec. 1 st. at each end of next row, then work 3 rows.

Rep. the last 4 rows 4(3:3:2:2) times more. [55(61:65:71:75) sts.]

Dec. 1 st. at each end of next and every alt. row until 21(21:23:23:25) sts. rem. ending with a wrong side row.

Leave sts. on holder.

FRONT

Work as for back as far as armholes, ending with 4th row.

Shape Raglan and Divide for Neck

Cast off 3 sts. at beg. of next 2 rows.

Next row: patt. 32(34:36:38:40), turn and leave rem. sts. on spare needle.

Next row: patt. to end.

Dec. 1 st. at each end of next row, then work 3 rows.

Cont. to dec. at neck edge on every 6th row until 8(8:9:9:10) sts. in all have been dec. at this edge.
AT THE SAME TIME cont. to dec. at armhole edge on next row and on every foll. 4th row 3(2:2:1:1) times more, then on every alt. row until 2 sts. rem. ending with a wrong side row.
Cast off.
Return to sts. on spare needle.
Sl. 1st st. onto a safety pin for neck, rejoin yarn and patt. to end.
Cont. to match first side, reversing all shapings.

SLEEVES

Cast on 35(35:35:39:39) sts. with 5½mm. needles and A, and work in rib as for back for 7 cm. (2¾ in.) ending with 2nd row.
Change to 6½mm. needles and cont. in patt. as on back, inc. 1 st. at each end of 5th and every foll. 8th row until there are only 51(53:55:57:59) sts., then at each end of every 6th row until there are 55(57:59:61:63) sts.
Cont. without shaping until sleeve measures 46(47:48:49:50) cm. (18(18½: 18¾:19¼:19½) in.) from beg. ending with 4th row.

Shape Top

Cast off 3 sts. at beg. of next 2 rows, then work 2 rows.
Dec. 1 st. at each end of next row, then work 3 rows.
Rep. the last 4 rows 5 times more.
Dec. 1 st. at each end of next and every alt. row until 9 sts. rem., ending with a wrong side row.
Leave sts. on holder.

NECKBAND

Sew up raglan seams.

With set of 4 5½mm. needles and A, k. sts. of back neck and left sleeve, knitting 2 tog. at seam, pick up 25(27:29:31:33) sts. down left front neck, k. centre front st. from safety pin, pick up 25(27:29:31:33) sts. up right front neck, then k. sts. of right sleeve, knitting last st. of sleeve tog. with first st. of back neck.
[88(92:98:102:108) sts.]
Next round: work in k.1, p.1 rib to 2 sts. before centre front, k.2 tog., p.1, sl.1, k.1, p.s.s.o., rib to end.
Rep. this round for 3 cm. (1 in.).
Cast off in rib, still dec. at centre front.

MAKING UP

Press according to instructions on ball band.
Sew up side and sleeve seams.
Press seams.

Tweedy Polo-neck Cable Sweater 1980

Chunky, hip-length polo-neck sweater in reversed stocking stitch with simple cable pattern on upper parts of body and raglan sleeves

★ Suitable for beginners

MATERIALS

Yarn
Pingouin Iceberg
19(21) × 50g. balls
or
Pingouin Pingoland
19(21) × 50g. balls

Needles
1 pair 5mm.
1 pair 6½mm.
1 cable needle
1 stitch holder

MEASUREMENTS

Bust
82–87(92–97) cm.
32–34(36–38) in.

Length
67 cm.
26¼ in.

TENSION

16 sts. and 16 rows = 10 cm. (4 in.) square over stocking stitch on 6½mm. needles. If your tension square does not correspond to these measurements, adjust the needle size used.

ABBREVIATIONS

k.=knit; p.=purl; st(s).=stitch(es); inc.= increase; dec.=decrease; beg.=begin(ning); rem. = remain(ing); rep. = repeat; alt. = alternate; tog. = together; sl. = slip stitch (transfer one stitch from left needle, knit-wise unless otherwise stated, to right hand needle.); cont. = continue; patt. = pattern; foll. = following; folls. = follows; mm. = millimetres; cm. = centimetre(s); in. = inch(es); rev.st.st. = reverse stocking stitch, (i.e. right side purl, wrong side knit); p.s.s.o. = pass the slip stitch over; cable twist = on rows indicated, work k.6 sections: sl.3 onto cable needle, leave at front of work, k.3, k.3 from cable needle.

BACK

Cast on 82(86) sts. with 5mm. needles.

Work in k.1, p.1 rib for 13 cm. (5 in.).
Change to 6½mm. needles and rev.st.st.
NB. purl is right side of work.
Work straight for 25 cm. (9¾ in.) (total length of work 38 cm. (15 in.)).
Start cable pattern:
1st row: p.10(12), * k.6, p.8, k.6, p.8, k.6, p.8, k.6, p.8, k.6, * p.10(12).
2nd row: k.10(12), * p.6, k.8, p.6, k.8, p.6, k.8, p.6, k.8, p.6, * k.10(12).

Shape Raglan Armhole

3rd row: cast off 3(5) sts., p.6(6), work as for 1st row from * to *, p.10(12).
4th row: cast off 3(5) sts., k.6(6), work as for 2nd row from * to *, k.7(7).
5th row: p.2, sl.1, p.1, p.s.s.o., work in patt. as before to last 4 sts., p.2 tog., p.2.
6th row: as work faces you, k. all knit sts., p. all p. sts.
Continue working rows 5 and 6 to neck, with the exception of rows 7, 19, 31 and 43 where the k.6 section should be twisted for the cable, (see abbreviations).

Shape Neckline

47th row: k.6, turn, work 2 sts. tog. at neck edge on next 3 alt. rows, cast off.
Leave centre 22 sts. on stitch holder.
Rejoin yarn to shoulder edge of work.
Work 1 row. Work 2 sts. tog. at beg. of next and foll. 2 alt. rows.
Cast off.

FRONT

Work as for back.

SLEEVES

Cast on 44 sts. with 5mm. needles.
Work in k.1, p.1 rib for 13 cm. (5 in.).
Change to 6½mm needles and rev.st.st.
Inc. 1 st. at beg. and end of every 10th row until there are 52 sts.
Work straight until total work length is 46 cm. (18 in.).
Start cable patt. at right side: p.9, k.6, p.8, k.6, p.8, k.6, p.9.
Next row: k.9, p.6, k.8, p.6, k.8, p.6, k.9.
Now work dec. and patt. as in rows 5 and 6 of back, working cable twist on 7th and every foll. 12th row, until 10 sts. rem.
Now dec. at beg. and end of every row 4 times.
k.2 tog., fasten off.

POLO NECK

Join right shoulder seam.
Starting at left shoulder pick up, on 5mm. needles, 7 sts. down left side of neck, 22 sts. across front, 14 sts. around right side of neck, 22 sts. across back, 7 sts. up left side of neck. [72 sts.]
Work in k.1, p.1 rib for 24 cm. (9½ in.).
Cast off loosely in rib.

MAKING UP

DO NOT PRESS.
Sew polo-neck seam.
Sew in raglan sleeves.
Sew side seams.

Norwegian Sweater

Two-tone, hip-length, stocking stitch sweater with raglan sleeves, firm-rib welts, and patterned yoke knitted in the round

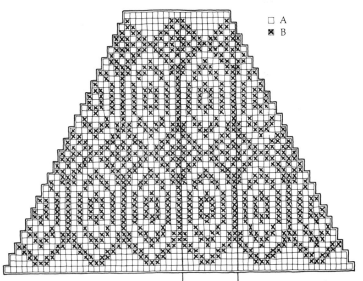

□ A
☒ B

10 st. rep. patt.

★ Suitable for adventurous beginners

MATERIALS

Yarn
Phildar Sagittaire
8(8:9:9:10:10:11) × 50g. balls (Col. A)
1(1:1:1:1:2:2) × 50g. balls (Col. B)

Needles
1 pair 3mm.
1 pair 3¾mm.
1 circular 3¾mm.
1 set of 4 double-pointed 3mm.

MEASUREMENTS

Bust
82(87:92:97:102:107:112) cm.
32(34:36:38:40:42:44) in.

Length
64(65:66:67:68:69:70) cm.
25(25½:26:26¼:26¾:27¼:27½) in.

Sleeve Seam
45(45:46:46:47:47:47) cm.
17¾(17¾:18:18:18½:18½:18½) in.

TENSION

22 sts. and 32 rows = 10 cm. (4 in.) square
over st.st. on 3¾mm. needles. If your tension square does not correspond to these
measurements, adjust the needle size
used.

ABBREVIATIONS

k.=knit; p.=purl; st(s).=stitch(es); inc.=
increase; dec.=decrease; beg.=begin(ning);
rem. = remain(ing); rep. = repeat; alt. =
alternate; tog. = together; sl. = slip stitch
(transfer one stitch from left needle, knitwise unless otherwise stated, to right
hand needle.); cont. = continue; patt. =
pattern; foll. = following; folls. = follows;
mm. = millimetres; cm. = centimetres; in.
= inch(es); st.st. = stocking stitch.

BACK

Cast on 102(106:112:118:124:128:134) sts.
with 3mm. needles and A.
Work 6 cm. (2¼ in.) in k.1, p.1, rib and inc.
1 st. at end of last row. [103(107:113:119:
125:129:135) sts.]
Change to 3¾mm. needles and cont. in
st.st. until work measures 42(43:44:44:44:
45:45) cm. (16½(16¾:17¼:17¼:17¼:17¾:
17¾) in.), ending with a wrong side row.

Shape Raglan

Cast off 3(4:4:5:6:5:6) sts. at beg. of next 2
rows.

Dec. 1 st. at each end of next and every alt.
row until 73(73:83:83:93:93) sts. rem.
P.1 row. Leave sts. on a spare needle.

FRONT

Work as for back until front matches back
to armholes, ending with a wrong side
row.

Shape Raglan And Yoke Curve

Cast off 3(4:4:5:6:5:6) sts. at beg. of next 2
rows.
Dec. 1 st. at each end of next and every alt.
row until 89(89:99:99:99:109:109) sts. rem.
P.1 row.
1st row: k.2 tog., k.34(34:39:39:39:44:44),
turn, leave rem. sts.
2nd and alt. rows: p. to end.
3rd row: k.2 tog., k.29(29:33:33:33:37:37),
turn.
5th row: k.2 tog., k.24(24:27:27:27:30:30),
turn.
7th row: k.2 tog., k.19(19:21:21:21:23:23),
turn.
9th row: k.2 tog., k.14(14:15:15:15:16:16),
turn.
11th row: k.2 tog., k.9, turn.
13th row: k.2 tog., k.4, turn.
15th row: k.2 tog., cont. across all sts., k. to
last 2 sts., k.2 tog.
Next row: p.35(35:40:40:40:45:45), turn.
Cont. to dec. 1 st. at raglan edge and to

work curve to match other side, reversing shaping, until 13th row has been worked.
Next row: p. across all sts. [73(73:83:83:83: 93:93) sts.]
Leave sts. on a spare needle.

SLEEVES

Cast on 52(54:56:60:62:62:64) sts. with 3mm. needles and A.
Work 8 cm. (3¼ in.) in k.1, p.1, rib and inc. 1 st. at end of last row. [53(55:57: 61:63:63: 65) sts.]
Change to 3¾mm. needles, cont. in st.st. Inc. 1 st. at each end of 7th and every foll. 8th row until there are 75(69:67:71:75:75: 77) sts. and then every foll. 6th row until there are 83(87:91:95:97:97:99) sts.
Work straight until sleeve measures 45(45: 46:46:47:47:47) cm. (17¾(17¾:18:18:18½: 18½:18½) in.)

Shape Raglan

Cast off 3(4:4:5:6:5:6) sts. at beg. of next 2 rows. Work 2 rows.
Dec. 1 st. at each end of next and every foll. 4th row 4(4:0:1:3:0:2) times more. [67(69:81:81:77:85:81) sts.]
Dec. 1 st. at each end of every alt. row until 63 sts. rem.
P.1 row. Leave sts. on a spare needle.

YOKE

With 3¾mm. circular needle and right side of work facing, work across 73(73:83: 83:83:93:93) sts. from back following chart thus: ** k.2 tog. A, k.3 A, * k.3 B, k.7 A, rep. from * to last 8 sts., k.3 B, k.3 A, k.2 tog. A, ** place coloured thread to mark dec. point, rep. from ** to ** across 63 sts. for sleeve, rep. from ** to ** across 73(73: 83:83:83:93:93) sts. for front, and rep. again

across 63 sts. for other sleeve, placing markers between each dec. point.
Cont. in rounds, following patt. from chart and dec. 1 st. each side of markers every alt. round as shown on chart.
Complete chart. [96(96:116:116:136: 136) sts.]
Cont. in A and cont. to dec. as before on alt. rounds 0(0:2:1:0:2:2) times more. [96(96:100:108:116:120:120) sts.]
Change to set of 4 double-pointed 3mm. needles, arrange sts. on 3 needles and cont. in k.1, p.1 rib.
Work 12 rounds.
Cast off loosely in rib.

MAKING UP

Sew up raglan seams.
Sew up side and sleeve seams.
Press lightly on wrong side.

Shawl-collared Mohair Cardigan 1959

Soft, loose-fitting mohair cardigan in twisted rib, with knitted-in front bands, shawl collar and doubled border mitred into fronts

** Suitable for knitters with some previous experience

MATERIALS

Yarn
Lister Lee Tahiti
20(21:22:23:24) × 25g. balls

Needles
1 pair 3¼mm.
1 pair 4mm.
1 pair 6mm.

Buttons
6

MEASUREMENTS

Bust
82(87:92:97:102) cm.
32(34:36:38:40) in.

Length
62(65:67:70:71) cm.
24¼(25½:26¼:27½:27¾) in.

Sleeve Seam (with cuff turned back)
46 cm.
(18 in.)

TENSION

8 sts. and 11 rows = 5 cm. (2 in.) square over stocking stitch on 6mm. needles. If your tension square does not correspond to these measurements, adjust the needle size used.

ABBREVIATIONS

k.=knit; p.=purl; st(s).=stitch(es); inc.= increase; dec.=decrease; beg.=begin(ning); rem. = remain(ing); rep. = repeat; alt. = alternate; tog. = together; sl. = slip stitch (transfer one stitch from left needle, purl-wise, to right hand needle); cont. = continue; patt. = pattern; foll. = following; folls. = follows; mm. = millimetres; cm. = centimetre(s); in. = inch(es); p.s.s.o. = pass slipped st. over; k.1b. = knit into back of st.

BACK

Cast on 77(81:85:89:93) sts. with 4½mm. needles.
1st row (right side): k.1b., *p.1, k.1b., rep. from * to end.
2nd row: p.
These 2 rows form patt., rep. until work measures 5 cm. (2 in.), ending with 2nd row, then change to 6mm. needles and cont. in patt. until back measures 37(37:36: 36:34) cm. (14½:14½:14:14:13¼) in.) at centre from start, ending with right side facing.

Shape Raglans

Cast off 4 sts. at beg. of next 2 rows.
1st row: (k.1b., p.1) 3 times, sl.1, k.1, p.s.s.o., patt. to last 8 sts., k.2 tog., (p.1, k.1b.) 3 times.
2nd row: p.
3rd row: (k.1b., p.1) 3 times, k.1, patt. to last 7 sts., k.1, (p.1, k.1b.) 3 times.
4th row: p.
Rep. last 4 rows 2(4:6:8:10) times more. [63 sts.]

Now rep. 1st and 2nd rows until 21(23:25:27:29) sts. rem. ending with 2nd row.
Cast off.

LEFT FRONT

Cast on 51(53:55:57:59) sts. with 4½mm. needles.
1st row: * k.1 b., p.1, rep. from * to last 15 sts., k.1 b., k.14.
2nd row: p.
Rep. last 2 rows until work measures 5 cm. (2 in.), ending with 2nd row.
Change to 6mm. needles and, keeping 15 sts. at front edge in st.st., cont. in rib patt. until front matches back side edge, ending with right side facing.

Shape Raglan

Cast off 4 sts. at beg. of next row. Work 1 row straight.
1st row: (k.1 b., p.1) 3 times, sl.1, k.1, p.s.s.o., patt. to last 15 sts., k.1 b., k.14.
2nd row: p.
3rd row: (k.1 b., p.1) 3 times, k.1, patt. to last 15 sts., k.1 b., k.14.
4th row: p.
Work rows 1–3 inclusive again.
With wrong side facing, shape front edging as folls.:
1st row: p.7 sts., turn.
2nd row: k.2 tog., k.5.
Cont. on these 6 sts., dec. 1 st. at beg. of every foll. alt. row until all sts. are gone.
With wrong side facing, rejoin yarn to rem. 38(40:42:44:46) sts., p. to end.
Dec. 1 st. at front edge on next and every foll. alt. row and at the same time cont. dec. at raglan edge on next and every foll. 4th row until 33(29:25:24:28) sts. rem.
Work 1 (1:1:3:1) rows straight.
Cont. as folls.:
5th size only: cont. dec. at raglan edge as before on next and every foll. 4th row and at the same time dec. 1 st. at front edge on every foll. 4th row from last dec., until 22 sts. rem.
Work 1 row straight.
1st size only: cont. dec. at raglan edge as before, but on the next and every alt. row and at the same time dec. 1 st. at front edge on next and every alt. row until 9 sts. rem.
2nd and 3rd sizes only: cont. dec. at raglan edge as before, but on next and every alt. row and at the same time dec. 1 st. at front edge on next and every alt. row until 17(19) sts. rem., then on every foll. 3rd(4th) row until 9 sts. rem.
4th and 5th sizes only: cont. dec. at raglan edge as before but on next and every alt. row and at the same time dec. 1 st. at front edge on every foll. 4th row from last dec., until 9 sts. rem.
All sizes:
Next row: p.
Next row: (k.1 b., p.1) 3 times, sl.1, k.2 tog., p.s.s.o.
Next row: p.
Next row: (k.1 b., p.1) twice, k.1 b., sl.1, k.1, p.s.s.o.
Next row: p.
Next row: (k.1 b., p.1) twice, sl.1, k.1, p.s.s.o.

Next row: p.
Cont. dec. at front edge on next and every alt. row until 2 sts. rem., p.2, turn.
k.2 tog. and fasten off.

RIGHT FRONT

Work to correspond with left front with the addition of 6 buttonholes.
Mark position of buttons on left front with pins to ensure even spacing, then work holes to correspond, 1st 2 cm. (1 in.) from lower edge and rest evenly spaced between.
To make a buttonhole (right side facing): k.2, cast off 3 sts., k.4, cast off 3 sts., k.2, patt. to end. Work back, casting on 3 sts. over those cast off.
NOTE: When shaping raglan work 'k.2 tog.' for 'sl.1, k.1, p.s.s.o.'.

LEFT SLEEVE

Cast on 43(45:47:49:51) sts. with 3¼mm. needles and work 7 cm. (2¾ in.) in st.st. ending with a p. row. Change to 6mm. needles and starting with 1st row, work in rib patt. as for back, shaping sides by inc. 1 st. at each end of 5th and every foll. 8th row until there are 63(65:67:69:71) sts., taking inc. sts. into patt.
Work straight until sleeve seam measures 49 cm. (19¼ in.), ending with right side facing.

Shape Raglans

Cast off 4 sts. at beg. of next 2 rows, then dec. 1 st. at each end of next and every foll. 4th row until 49(47:45:43:41) sts. rem.
Work 3 rows straight, then dec. as before, but on next and every alt. row until 15 sts. rem., ending with right side facing.
Cont. as folls.:
1st row: (k.1 b., p.1) 3 times, sl.1, k.2 tog., p.s.s.o., (p.1, k.1 b.) 3 times.
2nd row: p.
3rd row: (k.1 b., p.1) twice, k.1 b., p.3 tog., (k.1 b., p.1) twice, k.1 b.
4th row: cast off 3 sts., p. to end.
5th row: (k.1 b., p.1) 3 times, sl.1, k.1, p.s.s.o.
6th row: as 4th.
7th row: (k.1 b., p.1) twice.
8th row: as 2nd.
Cast off.

RIGHT SLEEVE

Work to correspond with left sleeve, reversing top shaping.

COLLAR

Cast on 95(99:103:107:111) sts. with 6mm. 6mm. needles, and starting with 1st row, work in rib patt. as for back, shaping collar as folls.:
1st row: patt. 57(61:65:69:73) sts., turn.
2nd row: sl.1, p.18(22:26:30:34), turn.
3rd row: sl.1, patt. 21(25:29:33:37) sts., turn.
4th row: sl.1, p.5, * (p. into front, back and front of next st.), p.5(7:9:11:13), rep. from

* once more, (p. into front, back and front of next st.), p.6, turn. [101(105:109:113: 117) sts.]
5th row: sl.1, patt. 33(37:41:45:49) sts., turn.
6th row: sl.1, p.36(40:44:48:52), turn.
7th row: sl.1, patt. 39(43:47:51:55) sts., turn.
8th row: sl.1, p.5, * (p. into front, back and front of next st.), p.7(9:11:13:15), (p. into front, back and front of next st.) *, p.13, rep. from * to *, p.6, turn. [109(113:117: 121:125) sts.]
9th row: sl.1, patt. 53(57:61:65:69) sts., turn.
Cont. working 3 sts. more on every row until the row 'sl.1, patt. 98(102:106:110: 114) sts., turn' has been worked. Now work 1 st. more on every row until all sts. are worked.
Cast off purlwise.

Border

Cast on 2 sts. with 4½mm. needles. Starting with a k. row, cont. in st.st., shaping mitre by inc. 1 st. at each end of next and every alt. row until there are 14 sts.
Work straight until border fits from last inc. round outer edge of collar, ending with a p. row. Now dec. 1 st. at each end of next and every alt. row until 2 sts. rem.
Cast off.

MAKING UP

Press work very lightly on wrong side, taking care not to spoil the patt.
Sew up raglan, side and sleeve seams.
Pin cast on edge of collar round neck, sew in position.
Pin border round collar, right side of collar to right side of border, sew in position, then fold borders to wrong side and slip-hem lightly in position all round.
Fold cuffs in half to wrong side and finish as for borders.
Oversew loosely round double button-holes. Press all seams. Sew on buttons.

Mohair Sweater with Ribbed Collar

Soft, hemmed, hip-length sweater with large ribbed and rolled collar and set-in sleeves, in slipped stocking stitch

★★ Suitable for knitters with some previous experience

MATERIALS

Yarn
Hayfield Lugano Mohair
7(7:7:8) × 50g. balls

Needles
1 pair 4½mm.
1 pair 5½mm.
1 pair 6½mm.

MEASUREMENTS

Bust
82(87:92:97) cm.
32(34:36:38) in.

Length
59(60:61:62) cm.
23¼(23½:24:24¼) in.

Sleeve Seam
44 cm.
17¼ in.

TENSION

20 sts. and 32 rows = 10 cm. (4 in.) square over pattern on 5½mm. needles. If your tension square does not correspond to these measurements, adjust the needle size used.

ABBREVIATIONS

k.=knit; p.=purl; st(s).=stitch(es); inc.= increase; dec.=decrease; beg.=begin(ning); rem. = remain(ing); rep. = repeat; alt. = alternate; tog. = together; sl. = slip stitch (transfer one stitch from left needle, knitwise unless otherwise stated, to right hand needle.); cont. = continue; patt. = pattern; foll. = following; folls. = follows; mm. = millimetres; cm. = centimetre(s); in. = inch(es); st.st. = stocking stitch.

BACK

Cast on 87(91:97:101) sts. with 4½mm. needles and beg. with a k. row, work 10 rows in st.st.
Change to 5½mm. needles and cont. in patt. as folls.:
1st row: k. to end.
2nd row: p.1, * sl.1 purlwise, p.1, rep. from * to end.
These 2 rows form the patt. and are rep. throughout.
Cont. in patt., inc. 1 st. at each end of next and every foll. 12th row until there are 97(101:107:111) sts., then cont. without shaping until work measures 42 cm. (16½ in.) from beg., ending with a p. row.

Shape Armholes
Still working in patt., cast off 3(4:5:6) sts. at beg. of next 2 rows, then dec. 1 st. at each end of next 3 rows and every alt. row until 73(75:77:79) sts. rem.
Cont. straight until armholes measure 17(18:19:20) cm. (6½(7:7½:7¾) in.).

Shape Shoulders
Cast off 5(6:6:7) sts. at beg. of next 4 rows, then 6(5:6:5) sts. at beg. of next 2 rows.
Cast of rem. 41 sts. loosely.

FRONT

Work as given for back until armholes measure 8 rows less than on back, ending with a p. row.

Shape Neck
Next row: k.28(29:30:31), cast off 17 sts., k. to end.
Cont. on last set of sts.
Dec. 1 st. at neck edge on every row until 20(21:22:23) sts. rem., ending at armhole edge.

Shape Shoulder
Next row: cast off (5:6:6:7) sts., patt. to last 2 sts., p.2 tog.
Next row: k.2 tog., k. to end.
Rep. the last 2 rows once more, then cast off rem. 6(5:6:5) sts.
Return to the other set of sts. and work to match, reversing shaping.

SLEEVES

Cast on 51(53:55:57) sts. with 4½mm. needles.
1st row: k.1, * p.1, k.1, rep. from * to end.
2nd row: p.1, * k.1, p.1, rep. from * to end.
Rep. these 2 rows for 7 cm. (2¾ in.), ending with a 2nd row.
Change to 5½mm. needles and cont. in patt. as on back, inc. 1 st. at each end of 11th and every foll. 6th row until there are 69(73:77:81) sts., then cont. without shaping until sleeve seam measures 44 cm. (17¼ in.) from beg., or length required, ending with a p. row.

Shape Top
Cast off 4(5:6:7) sts. at beg. of next 2 rows.
Dec. 1 st. at each end of next and every alt. row until 41 sts. rem., then at each end of every row until 17 sts. rem.
Cast off.

COLLAR

Cast on 18 sts. with 6½mm. needles and 2 strands of yarn, and p. 1 row.
Next row: * k.1, k. into loop below next st. and sl. the st. off needle, rep. from * to end. This row forms the patt. and is rep. throughout.
Work 3 more rows.
** *Next row:* patt. to last 4 sts., turn and patt. to end.
Work 2 complete rows.
Next row: patt. to last 6 sts., turn and patt. to end.
Work 2 complete rows. **
Rep. from ** to ** until shorter edge measures 60 cm. (23½ in.). Cast off in patt.

MAKING UP

Do not press.
Sew up shoulder seams.
Sew in sleeves.
Sew up side and sleeve seams.
Turn up hem at lower edge and slipstitch.
Sew up cast on and cast off edges of collar, then sew shorter edge of collar to neck, with seam at centre back.

Alpaca Socks with Clocks

Furry, ankle-length socks in stocking stitch with Swiss-embroidered contrast side clocks, ribbed heel and top welt

★★ Suitable for knitters with some previous experience

MATERIALS

Yarn
Jaeger Alpaca
2(2:3) × 50g. balls (Main Col. A)
1(1:1) × 50g. ball (Contrast Col. B)

Needles
1 set of 4 double-pointed 2¾mm.

MEASUREMENTS

Length of Foot
24(27:28) cm.
9½(10½:11) in.

Length from Top to Base of Heel
41 cm.
16 in.

TENSION

32 sts. and 40 rows = 10 cm. (4 in.) square over st.st. on 2¾mm. needles. If your tension square does not correspond to these measurements, adjust the needle size used.

ABBREVIATIONS

k.=knit; p.=purl; st(s).=stitch(es); inc.= increase; dec.=decrease; beg.=begin(ning); rem. = remain(ing); rep. = repeat; alt. = alternate; tog. = together; sl. = slip stitch (transfer one stitch from left needle, knitwise unless otherwise stated, to right hand needle).; cont. = continue; patt. = pattern; foll. = following; folls. = follows; mm. = millimetres; cm. = centimetres; in. = inch(es); st.st. = stocking stitch; p.s.s.o. = pass the slipped st. over; tbl. = through back of loop; m.1 = make 1 st.: pick up horizontal loop lying before next st. and work into back of it; sl.1K = sl. 1 st. knitwise; sl.1P = sl. 1 st. purlwise.

Cast on 68 sts.: 24 sts. on each of 1st and 3rd needles, and 20 sts. on 2nd needle. Work in rounds of k.2, p.2 rib for 8 cm. (3¼ in.).
Next round: (k.17, m.1) 4 times. [72 sts.]
Place a coloured marker at end of last round to mark centre back.
Work in patt. as folls.:

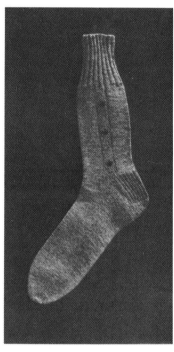

☑ B, darned

Next round: k.16, p.1, k.6, p.1, k.24, p.1, k.6, p.1, k.16.
Rep. this round until work measures 20 cm. (7¾ in.).

Shape Leg
1st round: k.1, k.2 tog., patt. to last 3 sts., sl. 1K, k.1, p.s.s.o., k.1.
Work 2nd to 6th rounds in patt.
Rep. last 6 rounds 5 times more. [60 sts.]
Work straight until work measures 33 cm. (13 in.).

Divide for Heel
Next round: k.14, sl. last 15 sts. of round onto end of same needle, (these 29 sts. are for heel).

Divide rem. sts. onto two needles and leave for instep.

Shape Heel
1st row: sl.1P, p. to end.
2nd row: sl. 1K, * k.1, keeping yarn at back of needle, sl.1P, rep. from * to last 2 sts., k.2.
Rep. last 2 rows 16 times more, then 1st row again.

Turn Heel
1st row: k.17, sl.1K, k.1, p.s.s.o., turn.
2nd row: p.6, p.2 tog., turn.
3rd row: k.7, sl.1K, k.1, p.s.s.o., turn.
4th row: p.8, p.2 tog., turn.
Cont. to dec. until all sts. are worked onto one needle.
Next row: k.9, thus completing heel (8 sts. rem. unworked on left hand needle).
Sl. all instep sts. onto one needle.
Using spare needle, k.8 heel sts. k. up 18 sts. along side of heel, using 2nd needle k. across instep sts., using 3rd needle k. up 18 sts. along other side of heel, k.9 heel sts. [84 sts.]

Shape Instep
1st round: k.
2nd round: 1st needle – k. to last 3 sts., k.2 tog., k.1.
2nd needle – k.
3rd needle – k.1, k.2 tog. tbl., k. to end.
Rep. these 2 rounds until 58 sts. rem.
Cont. on these sts. until foot measures 16(18:19) cm. (6¼(7:7½) in.) from where sts. were knitted up at heel.
Sl. 1st st. of 2nd needle onto end of 1st needle, and last st. of 2nd needle onto 3rd needle.

Shape Toe
1st round: 1st needle – k. to last 3 sts., k.2 tog. k.1.
2nd needle – k.1, k.2 tog. tbl., k. to last 3 sts., k.2 tog., k.1.
3rd needle – k.1, k.2 tog. tbl., k. to end.
2nd round: k.
Rep. these rounds until 26 sts. rem.
K. sts. from 1st needle onto end of 3rd needle.
Cast off sts. from two needles tog.: hold 2 needles parallel and cast off 1 st. from each needle alternately to end. With B, Swiss darn 3 stars as shown in chart between the p. sts. on side of socks.

High-neck Heart Pattern Sweater

1961

Simple, thick sweater, with four-coloured stocking stitch heart pattern, stand-up doubled collar, raglan sleeves and ribbed welts

★★ Suitable for knitters with some previous experience

MATERIALS

Yarn
Sunbeam Aran
12(12:13) × 50g. balls (Main Colour A) (Cream)
3(3:3) × 50g. balls (Contrast Colour B) (Navy)
2(3:3) × 50g. balls (Contrast Colour C) (Mid-Blue)
2(3:3) × 50g. balls (Contrast Colour D) (Grey)

Needles
1 pair 4mm.
1 pair 5mm.

MEASUREMENTS

Bust
87(92:97) cm.
34(36:38) in.

Length (from back neck)
64(66:66) cm.
25(26:26) in.

Sleeve Seam
43 cm.
16¾ in.

TENSION

10½ sts. and 10½ rows = 5 cm. (2 in.) square over pattern on 5mm. needles. If your tension square does not correspond to these measurements, adjust the needle size used.

ABBREVIATIONS

k.=knit; p.=purl; st(s).=stitch(es); inc.= increase; dec.=decrease; beg.=begin(ning); rem. = remain(ing); rep. = repeat; alt. = alternate; tog. = together; sl. = slip stitch (transfer one stitch from left needle, knitwise unless otherwise stated, to right hand needle.); cont. = continue; patt. = pattern; foll. = following; folls. = follows; mm. = millimetres; cm. = centimetre(s); in. = inch(es); A = A colour; B = B colour; C = C colour; D = D colour; st.st.= stocking stitch.

BACK

Cast on 84(90:90) sts. with 4mm. needles and A.

1st row: p.1(2:2), k.2, * p.2, k.2, rep. from * to the last 1(2:2) sts., p.1(2:2).
2nd row: k.1(2:2), p.2, * k.2, p.2, rep. from * to the last 1(2:2) sts., k.1(2:2).
Rep. 1st and 2nd rows for 12 cm. (4¾ in.), ending with 1st row.
Next row: p.1(4:4), p. into front and back of next st., * p.4(4:3), p. into front and back of next st., rep. from * to the last 2(5:5) sts., p. to end. [101(107:111) sts.]
Change to 5mm. needles.
Joining in and breaking off colours as required, cont. in st.st., working in patt. from chart No. 1 for 1st size, chart No. 2 for 2nd size, or chart No. 3 for 3rd size, rep. the 10 patt. sts. 10(10:11) times across, and working odd sts. as indicated.
Work until the 22nd(24th:22nd) row of the 2nd patt. from beg. has been completed.

Shape Raglan Armholes
Dec. 1 st. at each end of next 6(6:8) rows.
1st size only:
Next row: k.2 tog., work to last 2 sts, k.2 tog.
Next row: work to end.
All sizes:
1st row: k.2 tog., work to last 2 sts., k.2 tog.
2nd row: p.2 tog., work to last 2 sts., p.2 tog.
3rd row: work to end.
4th row: as 2nd row.
5th row: as 1st row.
6th row: work to end.
Rep. 1st. to 6th rows 6(7:7) times more.
Break yarn and leave 31 rem. sts. on a stitch holder.

FRONT

Work as back.

SLEEVES

Cast on 46 sts. with 4mm. needles and A.
1st row: * p.2, k.2, rep. from * to the last 2 sts., p.2.
2nd row: * k.2, p.2, rep. from * to the last 2 sts., k.2.
Rep. 1st and 2nd rows for 12 cm. (4¾ in.), ending with 1st row.
Next row: * p.2, p. into front and back of next st., rep. from * to the last st., p.1. [61 sts.]
Change to 5mm. needles.
Cont. in st.st., working in patt. from chart No. 1 for all sizes, but starting with 31st patt. row.
Work 4(2:4) rows.
Now working the new sts. in patt., inc. 1

st. at each end of next row, and then every 6th(5th:4th) row until there are 81(87:91) sts.
Work 5(3:3) rows, ending with same row as back at underarms.

Shape top
Dec. 1 st. at each end of next 6(6:8) rows.
1st size only:
Next row: k.2 tog., work to last 2 sts., k.2 tog.
Next row: work to end.
All sizes:
1st row: k.2 tog., work to last 2 sts., k.2 tog.
2nd row: p.2 tog., work to last 2 sts., p.2 tog.
3rd row: work to end.
4th row: as 2nd row.
5th row: as 1st row.
6th row: work to end.
Rep. 1st to 6th rows 6(7:7) times more.
Break yarn and leave 11 rem. sts. on a stitch holder.

COLLAR

Press each piece lightly with warm iron and damp cloth.

With wrong side of work facing, slip sts. from stitch holders on to a 5mm. needle in the foll. order: sts. of back, sts. of right sleeve, sts. of front, and sts. of left sleeve. Patt. to last st. of left sleeve, k. last st. of sleeve tog. with first st. of front, patt. to last st. of front, k. last st. tog. with first st. of right sleeve, patt. to last st. of sleeve, k. last st. of sleeve tog. with first st. of back, patt. to end. Cont. with A.
Next row: k.
Work 11 more rows.
Change to 4mm. needles.
k. next row on wrong side to mark hem line. Now work 12 rows in st.st., starting with a k, row. Cast off.

MAKING UP

Sew up raglan and collar seams.
Fold collar to wrong side at the hemline and slipstitch in position.
Sew up side and sleeve seams.
Press seams lightly.

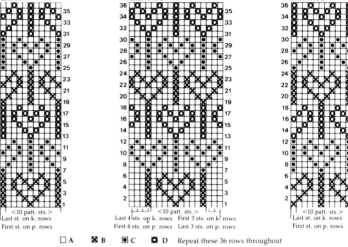

Chart No 1 — Chart No 2 — Chart No 3

Chart No 1: <10 patt. sts.> Last st. on k. rows / First st. on p. rows
Chart No 2: Last 4 sts. on k. rows First 3 sts. on k. rows / First 4 sts. on p. rows Last 3 sts. on p. rows / <10 patt. sts.>
Chart No 3: <10 patt. sts.> Last st. on k. rows / First st. on p. rows

□ A ☒ B ◉ C ◙ D   Repeat these 36 rows throughout

Turtle-neck, Leaf Pattern Sweater   1950

Thick, just below waist-length sweater with turtle-neck and set-in sleeves, in leaf pattern on garter stitch ground

★★ This pattern is suitable for knitters with some previous experience

MATERIALS

Yarn
Patons Clansman DK
9(9:10) × 50g. balls

Needles
1 pair 3mm.
1 pair 4mm.

MEASUREMENTS

Bust
87(92:97) cm.
34(36:38) in.

Length
48(49:51) cm.
18¾(19¼:20) in.

Sleeve Seam
46 (46:47) cm.
18(18:18½) in.

TENSION

10 sts. and 16 rows = 5 cm. (2 in.) square over stocking stitch on 4mm. needles. If your tension square does not correspond to these measurements, adjust the needle size used.

ABBREVIATIONS

k.=knit; p.=purl; st(s).=stitch(es); inc.= increase; dec.=decrease; beg.=begin(ning); rem. = remain(ing); rep. = repeat; alt. = alternate; tog. = together; sl. = slip stitch (transfer one stitch from left needle, purl-wise unless otherwise stated, to right hand needle.); cont. = continue; patt. = pattern; foll. = following; folls. = follows; mm. = millimetres; cm. = centimetre(s); in. = inch(es); m.1 = pick up horizontal loop lying before next stitch and work into back of it; L.1 = pick up horizontal loop lying before next stitch and knit it; p.s.s.o. = pass the slipped stitch over; 0 = no stitches; rev.st.st. = reversed stocking stitch i.e. right side purl.
NOTE: Where numbers of sts. are given, these refer to the basic number and do not include those made in the pattern.

BACK

** Cast on 83(89:95) sts. with 3mm. needles.
1st row (right side): k.1, * p.1, k.1, rep. from * to end.
2nd row: p.1, * k.1, p.1, rep. from * to end.
Rep. last 2 rows until work measures 9(10:11) cm. (3½(4:4¼) in.) at centre from start, ending with 1st row.
Next row: rib 3(6:3), m.1, * rib 7(7:8), m.1, rep. from * to last 3(6:4) sts., rib 3(6:4), [95(101:107) sts.]
Change to 4mm. needles.
Next row: p.
Next row: k.
Rep. last 2 rows once more.
Now work in patt.
1st row (right side): p.7(10:13), * L.1, k.1, L.1, p.15, rep. from * to last 8(11:14) sts. L.1, k.1, L.1, p.7(10:13).
2nd row: k.7(10:13), * p.3, k.15, rep. from * to last 10(13:16) sts., p.3, k.7(10:13).
3rd row: p.7(10:13), * L.1, k.3, L.1, p.15, rep. from * to last 10(13:16) sts., L.1, k.3, L.1, p.7(10:13).
4th row: k.7(10:13), * p.5, k.15, rep. from * to last 12(15:18) sts., p.5, k.7(10:13).
5th row: p.7(10:13), * L.1, k.1, sl.1, k.1, p.s.s.o., k.2, L.1, p.15, rep. from * to last 12(15:18) sts., L.1, k.1, sl.1, k.1, p.s.s.o., k.2, L.1, p.7(10:13).
6th row: k.7(10:13), * p.6, k.15, rep. from * to last 13(16:19) sts., p.6, k.7(10:13).
7th row: p.7(10:13), * L.1, k.2, sl.1, k.1, p.s.s.o., k.2, L.1, p.15, rep. from * to last 13(16:19) sts., L.1, k.2, sl.1, k.1, p.s.s.o., k.2, L.1, p.7(10:13).
8th row: k.7(10:13), * p.7, k.15, rep. from *

to last 14(17:20) sts., p.7, k.7(10:13).

9th row: p.7(10:13), * L.1, k.3, sl.1, k.1, p.s.s.o., k.2, L.1, p.15, rep. from * to last 14(17:20) sts., L.1, k.3, sl.1, k.1, p.s.s.o., k.2, L.1, p.7(10:13).

10th row: k.7(10:13), * p.8, k.15, rep. from * to last 15(18:21) sts., p.8, k.7(10:13).

11th row: p.7(10:13), * k.4, sl.1, k.1, p.s.s.o., k.2, p.15, rep. from * to last 15(18:21) sts., k.4, sl.1, k.1, p.s.s.o., k.2, p.7(10:13).

12th row: k.7(10:13), * p.7, k.15, rep. * to last 14(17:20) sts., p.7, k.7(10:13).

13th row: p.7(10:13), * sl.1, k.1, p.s.s.o., k.1, sl.1, k.1, p.s.s.o., k.2 tog., p.15, rep. from * to last 14(17:20) sts., sl.1, k.1, p.s.s.o., k.1, sl.1, k.1, p.s.s.o., k.2 tog., p.7(10:13).

14th row: k.7(10:13), * p.4, k.15, rep. * to last 11(14:17) sts., p.4, k.7(10:13).

15th row: p.7(10:13), * sl.1, k.1, p.s.s.o., k.2 tog., p.15, rep. from * to last 11(14:17) sts., sl.1, k.1, p.s.s.o., k.2 tog., p.7(10:13).

16th row: k.7(10:13), * p.2 tog., k.15, rep. from * to last 9(12:15) sts., p.2 tog., k.7(10:13).

17th and 19th rows: p.

18th and 20th rows: k.

21st row: p.0(3:6), * p.15, L.1, k.1, L.1, rep. from * to last 15(18:21) sts., p.15 (18:21).

22nd row: k.0(3:6), * k.15, p.3, rep. from * to last 15(18:21) sts., k.15(18:21).

23rd row: p.0(3:6), * p.15, L.1, k.3, L.1, rep. from * to last 15(18:21) sts., p.15(18:21).

24th row: k.0(3:6), * k.15, p.5, rep. from * to last 15(18:21) sts., k.15(18:21).

25th row: p.0(3:6), * p.15, L.1, k.1, sl.1, k.1, p.s.s.o., k.2, L.1, rep. from * to last 15(18:21) sts., p.15(18:21).

26th row: k.0(3:6), * k.15, p.6, rep. from * to last 15(18:21) sts., k.15(18:21).

27th row: p.0(3:6), * p.15, L.1, k.2, sl.1, k.1, p.s.s.o., k.2, L.1, rep. from * to last 15(18:21) sts., p.15(18:21).

28th row: k.0(3:6), * k.15, p.7, rep. from * to last 15(18:21) sts., k.15(18:21).

29th row: p.0(3:6), * p.15, L.1, k.3, sl.1, k.1, p.s.s.o., k.2, L.1, rep. from * to last 15(18:21) sts., p.15(18:21).

30th row: k.0(3:6), * k.15, p.8, rep. from * to last 15(18:21) sts., k.15(18:21).

31st row: p.0(3:6), * p.15, k.4, sl.1, k.1, p.s.s.o., k.2, rep. from * to last 15(18:21) sts. k.15(18:21).

32nd row: k.0(3:6), * k.15, p.7, rep. from * to last 15(18:21) sts., k.15(18:21).

33rd row: p.0(3:6), * p.15, sl.1, k.1, p.s.s.o., k.1, sl.1, k.1, p.s.s.o., k.2 tog., rep. from * to last 15(18:21) sts., p.15(18:21).

34th row: k.0(3:6), * k.15, p.4, rep. from * to last 15(18:21) sts., k.15(18:21).

35th row: p.0(3:6), * p.15, sl.1, k.1, p.s.s.o., k.2 tog., rep. from * to last 15(18:21) sts., p.15(18:21).

36th row: k.0(3:6), * k.15, p.2 tog., rep. from * to last 15(18:21) sts., k.15(18:21).

37th–40th rows: as 17th–20th.

These 40 rows form patt.

Patt. a further 20 rows straight.

Shape Armholes

Cont. in patt., casting off 6(6:7) sts. at beg. of next 2 rows, then dec. 1 st. at each end of next and every alt. row until 75(79:83) sts. rem. **

Work a further 47(47:49) rows straight in patt.

Shape Shoulders

Cont. in rev. st.st., casting off 9(8:9) sts. at beg. of next 2 rows, then 8(9:9) sts. at beg. of next 4 rows.

Leave rem. 25(27:29) sts. on a spare needle.

FRONT

Work as for back from ** to **.

Work a further 27 rows straight, thus ending with 16th(18th:18th) row of patt.

Shape Neck

Next row: p.28(29:30) sts., turn and leave rem. sts. on a spare needle.

Cont. on these 28(29:30) sts. for first side, dec. 1 st. at neck edge on every row until 25(26:27) sts. rem.

Working leaf at armhole edge only, cont. in patt. until front matches back to start of shoulder shaping, ending with right side facing.

Shape Shoulder

Cast off 9(8:9) sts. at beg. of next row, then 8(9:9) sts. at beg. of foll. 2 alt. rows.

With right side facing, slip centre 19(21:23) sts. onto a spare needle, rejoin yarn to rem. 28(29:30) sts., p. to end.

Finish to correspond with first side.

SLEEVES

Cast on 46(48:50) sts. with 3mm. needles.

Work 9(9:10) cm. (3½(3½:4) in.) in k.1, p.1 rib, inc. 1(3:5) sts. evenly across the last row. [47(51:55) sts.]

Change to 4mm. needles and patt. as for back. The first 2 rows will read:

1st row: p.7(9:11), * L.1, k.1, L.1, p.15, rep. from * to last 8(10:12) sts., L.1, k.1, L.1, p.7(9:11).

2nd row: k.7(9:11), * p.3, k.15, rep. from * to last 10(12:14) sts., p.3, k.7(9:11).

Cont. in patt. thus, shaping sides by inc. 1 st., at each end of 5th and every foll. 6th row until there are 73(77:81) sts., taking inc. sts. into patt.

Work 23 rows straight, thus ending with 20th patt. row.

Shape Top

Cast off 4(5:6) sts. at beg. of next 2 rows, then dec. 1 st. at each end of next and every alt. row until 47(49:51) sts. rem.

Cont. in rev. st.st., dec. 1 st. at each end of every foll. alt. row until 45 sts. rem.

Knit back, then dec. 1 st. at each end of every foll. alt. row until 31 sts. rem.

Cast off. rem. 13 sts.

NECK BORDER

Sew up right shoulder seam.

With right side facing and 3mm. needles, pick up and k.26 sts. down left side of neck, k.19(21:23) from centre, pick up and k.26 up right side, then k.25(27:29) from back. [96(100:104) sts.]

Work 9 cm. (3½ in.) in k.1, p.1 rib.

Cast off loosely in rib, using a bigger needle.

MAKING UP

Press work lightly on wrong side, omitting ribbing and taking care not to spoil the patt.

Sew up left shoulder seam, then sew up neck border with a flat seam.

Sew up side and sleeve seams; set in sleeves.

Press all seams.

Gathered Wool and Mohair Skirt

Simple skirt with hem, gathered into a waistband faced with ribbon and fastened with side zip, in twisted stocking stitch

★ Suitable for beginners

MATERIALS

Yarn
Pingouin Mohair 50
9(9:10:10) × 50g. balls

Needles
1 pair 5mm.
1 pair 5½mm.
3mm. crochet hook

Notions
18 cm. (7 in.) zip fastener
ribbon for facing, 2.5 cm. (1 in.) longer than your waist measurement

MEASUREMENT

Hip
87(92:97:102) cm.
34(36:38:40) in.

Length (completed including waistband)
69 cm.
27 in.

TENSION

17 sts. and 20 rows = 10 cm. (4 in.) square over twisted stocking stitch on 5½mm. needles. If your tension square does not correspond to these measurements, adjust the needle size used.

ABBREVIATIONS

k. = knit; p. = purl; st(s). = stitch(es); inc. = increase; dec. = decrease; beg. = begin(ning); rem. = remain(ing); rep. = repeat; alt. = alternate; tog. = together; sl. = slip stitch (transfer one stitch from left needle, knitwise unless otherwise stated, to right-hand needle.); cont. = continue; patt. = pattern; foll. = following; folls. = follows; mm. = millimetres; cm. = centimetre(s); in. = inch(es); t.b.l. = through back of loops.
NOTE: For twisted st.st. all sts. are worked through the back on the right side. Where instructions state 'k.' on the dec. rows, this means k. t.b.l.

BACK

Cast on 158(162:168:172) sts. with 5mm. needles.

Beg. with k. row, work 5 rows in st.st. for hem.
k. next row (wrong side) to make hemline ridge.
Change to 5½mm. needles and patt.
1st row: k. every st. t.b.l.
2nd row: k.1, p. to last st., k.1.
These 2 rows form patt.
Cont. until work measures 37 cm. (14½ in.) from hemline, ending with wrong side row.
1st dec. row: k.16(16:17:17), k.2 tog. t.b.l., (k.29(30:31:32), k.2 tog. t.b.l.) 4 times, k.16(16:17:17).
Cont. on rem. 153(157:163:167) sts. in patt. until work measures 45 cm. (17¾ in.) from hemline, ending with wrong side row.
2nd dec. row: k.15 (15:16:16), k.2 tog. t.b.l., (k.28(29:30:31), k.2 tog. t.b.l.) 4 times, k.16(16:17:17).
Cont. on rem. 148(152:158:162) sts. in patt. until work measures 53 cm. (20¾ in.) from hemline, ending with a wrong side row.
3rd dec. row: k.15(15:16:16) sts., k.2 tog. t.b.l., (k.27(28:29:30). k.2 tog., t.b.l.) 4 times, k.15(15:16:16) sts.
Cont. on rem. 143(147:153:157) sts. in patt. until work measures 61 cm. (24 in.) from hemline, ending with a wrong side row.
4th dec. row: k.14(14:15:15) sts., k.2 tog. t.b.l., (k.26(27:28:29), k.2 tog. t.b.l.) 4 times, k.15(15:16:16) sts.
Cont. on rem. 138(142:148:152) sts. in patt. until work measures 66 cm. (26 in.) from beg., ending with a wrong side row.
5th dec. row: k.1, * k.2 tog. t.b.l., rep. from * to last st., k.1. Now p. 1 row on rem. 70(72:75:77) sts., then cast off loosely.

FRONT

Work as for back.

MAKING UP

Backstitch the side seams, leaving left side open at top for 15 cm. (5¾ in.).
Fold up hem all around lower edge and slipstitch in place on wrong side.
Using crochet hook work double crochet around top of skirt for 2.5 cm. (1 in.). Fasten off.
Work 1 row of double crochet along both sides of opening. Cut ribbon to your waist measurement + 2.5 cm. (1 in.), and pin to inside of waist edge, easing in skirt to fit and folding under 1.25 cm. (½ in.) at each end.
Sew in place along upper edge and ends.
Sew zip into opening.
This garment can be brushed, very lightly, for a still softer effect.

Cosy, collared Ski Sweater

1960

Long, loose, ski sweater with huge, divided collar and set-in sleeves, knitted throughout in fisherman's rib

★★★ Suitable for experienced knitters

MATERIALS

Yarn
Patons Clansman DK
11(12:13:14) × 50g. balls

Needles
1 pair 3¼mm.
1 pair 4mm.

MEASUREMENTS

Bust
82(87:92:97) cm.
32(34:36:38) in.

Length
59(60:61:62) cm.
23¼(23½:24:24¼) in.

Sleeve Seam
36 cm.
14 in.

TENSION

18 sts. and 48 rows = 10 cm. (4 in.) square over patt. on 4mm. needles. If your tension square does not correspond to these measurements, adjust the needle size used.

ABBREVIATIONS

k.=knit; p.=purl; st(s).=stitch(es); inc.= increase; dec.=decrease; beg.=begin(ning); rem. = remain(ing); rep. = repeat; alt. = alternate; tog. = together; sl. = slip stitch (transfer one stitch from left needle, knit-wise unless otherwise stated, to right hand needle.); cont. = continue; patt. = pattern; foll. = following; folls. = follows; mm. = millimetres; cm. = centimetres; in. = inch(es); st.st. = stocking stitch; p.s.s.o. = pass the slipped st. over; k.1 blw. = k. 1 below: k. into next st. one row below, at the same time slipping off st. above.

BACK

** Cast on 70(74:76:80) sts. with 3¼mm. needles and work in fisherman's rib as folls.:
1st row (wrong side): k.
2nd row: * p.1, k.1 blw., rep. from * to last 2 sts., k.2.
Rep. 2nd row throughout.
Work straight for 7 cm. (2¾ in.).
Change to 4mm. needles and, keeping rib correct, shape sides by inc. 1 st. at each end of next and every foll. 6th row until there are 78(82:88:92) sts., taking inc. sts. into rib.
Work straight until back measures 45 cm. (17¾ in.).

Shape Armholes
Cast off 2 sts. at beg. of next 4 rows.
Dec. 1 st. at each end of next and every foll. alt. row until 58(64:68:74) sts. rem., ending with a wrong side row.
Dec. 1 st. at each end of next and every foll. 4th row until 42(44:48:50) sts. rem.
Work 3 rows. **
Dec. 1 st. at each end of next and every alt. row until 22(24:26:28) sts. rem., ending with a wrong side row.
Cast off rem. sts.

FRONT

Work as for back from ** to **.
Dec. 1 st. at each end of next and every foll. alt. row until 34(36:38:40) sts. rem., ending with a right side row.

Shape Neck
Next row: rib 14, cast off 6(8:10:12) sts., patt. to end.
Work left side first.
Dec. 1 st. at armhole and neck edge on next and every foll. alt. row until 2 sts. rem., ending with a wrong side row.
Cast off rem. 2 sts.

With right side facing, rejoin yarn to rem. sts. and complete to match first side, reversing shapings.

SLEEVES

Cast on 40(44:44:48) sts. with 3¼mm. needles and work in rib as given for back for 8 rows.
Change to 4mm. needles and shape sides by inc. 1 st. at each end of next and every foll. 10th(10th:8th:8th) row until there are 64(68:72:76) sts., taking inc. sts. into patt.
Work straight until sleeve seam measures 36 cm. (14 in.).

Shape Top
Cast off 2 sts. at beg. of next 4 rows.
Dec. 1 st. at each end of next and every foll. 4th row until 52(48:42:40) sts. rem.
Work 3 rows.
1st, 2nd and 3rd sizes:
Dec. 1 st. at each end of next and every foll. 6th row until 40 sts. rem.
Work 5 rows.

Shape Shoulder Dart
All sizes:
1st row: rib 19, sl.1, k.2 tog., p.s.s.o., patt. 18.
Work 4(4:6:6) rows.
Next row: rib 17, sl.1, k.2 tog., p.s.s.o., patt. 18.
Work 4(4:6:6) rows.
Next row: rib 17, sl.1, k.2 tog., p.s.s.o., patt. 16.
Work 4(4:6:6) rows.
Next row: rib 15, sl.1, k.2 tog., p.s.s.o., patt. 16.
Work 4 rows.
Cont. to dec. 2 sts. in centre on every 5th row until 18 sts. rem.
Cast off.

COLLAR

Cast on 114(118:122:126) sts. with 4mm. needles. Work in rib for 16 cm. (6¼ in.).
Cast off 6 sts. at beg. of next 8 rows.
Cast off rem. sts.

MAKING UP

Sew up shoulder seams and set in sleeves.
Sew up side and sleeve seams.
Turn in two sts. along straight edges of collar, and sew down rib on wrong side, pulling stitching tight to give a straight line.
Overlap ends of collar for 5 cm. (2 in.) and pin cast-off edge of collar to neck, placing overlap to centre front and easing collar to fit.
Sew collar to sweater.

Thick, Ribbed Sweater Dress

Chunky, knee-length, body-hugging simple dress with long, cuffed sleeves, polo collar and set-in sleeves, in single rib

★ Suitable for beginners

MATERIALS

Yarn
Robin Aran
19(20:22:23) × 50g. balls

Needles
1 pair 4mm.
1 pair 4½mm.

MEASUREMENTS

Bust
82(87:92:97) cm.
32(34:36:38) in.

Side Seam
84 cm.
33 in.

Length
104(105:105.5:106:5) cm.
40¾(41:41¼:41¾) in.

Sleeve Seam (excluding cuff)
43 cm.
16¼ in.

TENSION

22 sts. and 12 rows = 5 cm. (2 in.) square over single rib on 4½mm. needles. If your tension square does not correspond to these measurements, adjust the needle size used.

ABBREVIATIONS

k.=knit; p.=purl; st(s).=stitch(es); inc.= increase; dec.=decrease; beg.=begin(ning); rem. = remain(ing); rep. = repeat; alt. = alternate; tog. = together; sl. = slip stitch (transfer one stitch from left needle, knitwise unless otherwise stated, to right hand needle.); cont. = continue; patt. = pattern; foll. = following; folls. = follows; mm. = millimetres; cm. = centimetre(s); in. = inch(es); single rib = k.1, p.1 alternately.

BACK

Cast on 105(111:117:123) sts. with 4½mm. needles and work in single rib, beg. odd-numbered rows with k.1, and even-numbered rows with p.1 until work

measures 37 cm. (14½ in.) i.e. 88 rows, or 25 cm. (9¾ in.) less than required skirt length.
Cont. in rib, dec. 1 st. at each end of next and foll. 12th rows 6 times in all. [93 (99:105:111) sts.]
Mark each end of the last row with a thread to denote waist. ** Rib 49 rows, (adjust here if a different length from that above is required).

Shape Armholes

Cast off 3(4:5:6) sts. at the beg. of the next 2 rows, then dec. 1 st. at both ends of the next and 6 foll. right-side rows. [73(77: 81:85) sts.]
Work 28 rows straight.
Next row: rib 27(28:29:30) sts. and leave on a spare needle for left shoulder, rib 19(21:23:25) sts. and leave on a stitch holder for polo collar, rib to end and work on these 27(28:29:30) sts.

Shape Right Shoulder

1st row: cast off 8 sts. rib to last 2 sts., work 2 tog.
2nd row: work 2 tog., rib to end.
Rep. these 2 rows once. Cast off the rem. 7(8:9:10) sts.

Shape Left Shoulder

Rejoin yarn to right side of 27(28:29:30) sts. and rib to end, then work as given for the right shoulder.

FRONT

Work as given for back as far as ** then rib a further 43 rows, (or 6 rows less than those worked on back from waist to armholes if length has been adjusted). Work bust darts:
1st row: rib until 24 sts. rem., turn.
2nd row: sl.1, rib until 24 sts. rem., turn.
3rd and 4th rows: sl.1, rib until 16 sts. rem., turn.
5th and 6th rows: sl.1, rib until 8 sts. rem., turn.
7th row: sl.1, rib to end. Rib 5 rows more.

Shape Armholes

Follow instructions given for the armhole shaping for back, then on 73(77:81:85) sts.

which rem. after dec., rib 14(16:18:20) rows.

Shape Neck

Next row: rib 31(32:33:34) and leave these sts. on a spare needle for right shoulder, rib 11(13:15:17) sts. and leave these sts. on a stitch-holder for polo collar, rib to end and work on these 31(32:33:34) sts.

Shape Left Shoulder

Dec. 1 st. at neck edge on next 8 rows, [23(24:25:26) sts.]
Work 4 rows straight. Cast off 8 sts. at beg. of the next and foll. alt. row. Work 1 row, then cast off rem. 7(8:9:10) sts.

Shape Right Shoulder

With right side facing, rejoin yarn to neck edge of 31(32:33:34) sts. and rib to end, then work as given for left shoulder.

SLEEVES

Cast on 41(43:45:47) sts. with 4mm. needles and work 27 rows in single rib as given for back. Change to 4½mm. needles. Cont. in rib, inc. 1 st. at both ends of the next and every foll. 6th row 12(13:14:14) more times. [67(71:75:77) sts.]
Work 15(9:3:3) rows straight.

Shape Sleeve Top

Cast off 3(4:5:6) sts. at beg. of the next 2 rows, then dec. 1 st. at the beg. only of the next 18(20:22:22) rows. Cast off 2 sts. at the beg. of the next 4 rows, and 3 sts. at the beg. of the foll. 6 rows. Cast off rem. 17 sts.

POLO COLLAR

Sew up right shoulder seam. With right side of work facing, using 4mm. needles, pick up and k.21 sts. from left front neck edge, rib across 11(13:15:17) centre front sts. pick up and k.21 sts. from right front neck edge, 8 sts. from right back neck edge, rib across 19(21:23:25) centre back sts., pick up and k.8 sts. from left back neck edge. [88(92:96:100) sts.]
Beg. each row with k.1, work 17 rows in single rib. Change to 4½mm. needles and rib a further 18 rows. Cast off in rib.

MAKING UP

DO NOT PRESS.
Sew up left shoulder seam, cont. seam along ends of polo collar rows, reversing the top half for collar turn-back.
Sew sleeves into armholes then join side and sleeve seams.
Fold polo collar over to right side. Turn up sleeve cuffs for 5 cm. (2 in.).

Collarless Checked Mohair Coat 1963

Thigh-length, borderless coat with three-quarter length sleeves and neck facing, in checked stocking stitch pattern worked from chart

★★★ Suitable for experienced knitters

MATERIALS

Yarn
Hayfield Aspen Mohair
10(11) × 25g. balls in colour A
9(10) × 25g. balls in colour B

Needles
1 pair 10mm.

MEASUREMENTS

Bust
82–87(92–97) cm.
32–34(36–38) in.

Length (at centre back)
82(83) cm.
32¼(32½) in.

Sleeve Seam
36 cm.
14 in.

TENSION

13 sts. and 11 rows = 10 cm. (4 in.) square over pattern on 10mm. needles. If your tension square does not correspond to these measurements, adjust the needle size used.

ABBREVIATIONS

k.=knit; p.=purl; st(s).=stitch(es); inc.= increase; dec.=decrease; beg.=begin(ning); rem. = remain(ing); rep. = repeat; alt. = alternate; tog. = together; sl. = slip stitch (transfer one stitch from left needle, knit-wise unless otherwise stated, to right hand needle.); cont. = continue; patt. = pattern; foll. = following; folls. = follows; mm. = millimetres; cm. = centimetre(s); in. = inch(es); reqd. = required; st.st. = stocking stitch.
NOTE: Entire coat is in st.st. with check pattern worked from chart. (Carry yarn LOOSELY at back of work. When working more than 3 sts. weave yarn every 3rd or 4th st. to prevent long strands

BACK

Beg. at lower side of left sleeve.
With A cast on 3 sts. Join in B.
1st row: k.1A, 1B, (1A, 1B) into last st.
2nd row: p.1A, 1B, 2A, cast on 6 sts.
3rd row: k.(1A, 1B) 3 times, 1A, 2B, k. twice into last st. with B.
4th row: p.5B, (1A, 1B) 3 times, cast on 6 sts.
5th row: k.6B, (1A, 1B) 3 times, 1A, 3B, k. twice into last st. with B.
6th row: p.6B, (1A, 1B) twice, 1A, 7B, cast on 6 sts.
7th row: k.(1A, 1B) twice, 1A, 7B, (1A, 1B) 3 times, 1A, 4B, k. twice into last st. with B.

8th row: p.(1B, 1A) twice, 1B, 9A, (1B, 1A) twice, 1B, 6A, cast on 4 sts.

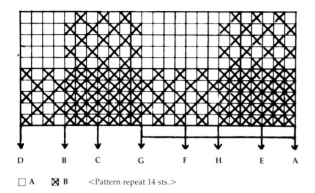

D   B   C   G   F   H   E   A

☐ A   ☒ B   <Pattern repeat 14 sts.>

Work 13 rows, ending with 4th row of patt. Break off yarn.
Work lower sleeve as for right sleeve of back to **.
Work across sts. of front. [92(99) sts.]
Inc. 1 st. at beg. of next 2 k. rows.
Work 1 row.

**** **Shape Upper Sleeve and Shoulder**
Cast off at beg. of next and foll. k. rows 3 sts. 9 times, 5 sts. 3 times, and 7 sts. once, ending at front edge. [45(52) sts.]

Shape Neck
1st row: cast off 12(10) sts., p. to end.
2nd row: cast off 7 sts., k. to last 2 sts., k.2 tog.
3rd row: p.2 tog., p. to end.
Rep. last 2 rows once (twice) more.
Next row: as 2nd. [7 sts.]
p. 1 row.
Cast off.

RIGHT FRONT

Follow instructions for left front, working k. rows from points E(F) to B once, then (H to B) 2(3) times and p. rows from (B to H) 2(3) times and B to E(F) once. Work dec. at end of rows instead of beg.
Work 12 rows after last dec., ending with a 3rd row.
For sleeve work as for left sleeve back to ***.
Now work across sts. of front. [91(98) sts.]
Inc. 1 st. at end of next 3 k. rows.
Now finish as for left front from ****, reading p. for k. and k. for p.

NECK FACING

Cast on 10 sts. with A.
1st row: k. twice into first st., k.7, k.2 tog.
2nd row: p. to end.
Rep. last 2 rows until band measures 38 cm.(15 in.) from cast on sts., ending with a p. row.
Next row: k.2 tog., k. to last 2 sts. k.2 tog.
Next row: p. to last 2 sts. p.2 tog.
Rep. last 2 rows until 2 sts. rem.
Cast off.

MAKING UP

Do not press.
Sew up shoulders. Sew up sleeve seams. Sew up side seams. Turn up 4 cm. (1½ in.) hems on sleeves and 4 rows at lower edge, slipstitch. Turn back 4 sts. down front edges and slipstitch. Sew facing to neck, right sides together, turn to wrong side and slipstitch.

9th row: k.1A, 1B, 7A, (1B, 1A) 3 times, 1B, 7A, (1B, 1A) twice, 1B, (1A, 1B) into last st.
10th row: p.(1A, 1B) 3 times, 9A, (1B, 1A), twice, 1B, 9A, 1B, cast on 4 sts.
11th row: * k.(1A, 1B) 3 times, 7A, 1B, rep. from * once more, (1A, 1B) twice, 1A, (1B, 1A) into last st.
12th row: p.2A, * (1B, 1A) twice, 1B, 9A, rep. from * once more, (1B, 1A) twice, 1B, cast on 4 sts.
13th row: k.1A, 1B, 1A, * 7B, (1A, 1B) 3 times, 1A, rep. from * once more, 7B, (1A, 1B) into last st.
14th row: * p.1A, 9B, (1A, 1B) twice, rep. from * once more, 1A, 9B, 1A, 1B, cast on 4 sts.
15th row: k. * (1A, 1B) 3 times, 1A, 7B, rep. from * twice more, 1A, (1A, 1B) into last st.
16th row: p.1B, 1A, * 9B, (1A, 1B) twice, 1A, rep. from * twice more, 1B, cast on 3 sts. [48 sts.] ***
Break yarn and leave sts. on spare needle.

Work Lower Back
Cast on 77(91) sts. with A.
p. 1 row. k. 1 row. p. 1 row.
Join in B and beg. working patt. from chart, working k. rows from point A and p. rows from point B. Work 20 rows.
Keeping patt. correct dec. 1 st. each end of next and every 10th row until 71(85) sts. rem.
Work 13 rows, ending with 4th row of patt.
Break yarn and leave sts. on spare needle.

Right Sleeve
Cast on 3 sts. with A.
1st row: k.(1B, 1A) into first st., 1B, 1A, cast on 6 sts.
2nd row: p.8A, 1B, 1A.

3rd row: k.2B into first st., 2B, (1A, 1B) 3 times, 1A, cast on 6 sts with B.
4th row: p.7B, (1A, 1B) twice, 1A, 5B.
5th row: k.2B into first st., 3B, (1A, 1B) 3 times, 1A, 6B, cast on 6 sts. with A, weaving B.
6th row: p.(1B, 1A) twice, 9B, (1A, 1B) twice, 1A, 6B.
7th row: k.2B into first st., 4B, (1A, 1B) 3

times, 1A, 7B, (1A, 1B) twice, 1A, cast on 4 sts.
8th row: p.1B, 9A, (1B, 1A) twice, 1B, 9A, (1B, 1A) twice, 1B.
9th row: k.(1B, 1A) into first st, (1B, 1A) twice, 1B, 7A, (1B, 1A) 3 times, 1B, 7A, 1B, 1A, cast on 4 sts.
10th row: p.(1B, 1A) twice, 1B, 9A, (1B, 1A) twice, 1B, 9A, (1B, 1A) 3 times.
11th row: k.(1A, 1B) into first st., (1A, 1B) 3 times, 7A, (1B, 1A) 3 times, 1B, 7A, (1B, 1A) 3 times, cast on 4 sts.
12th row: p.4A, (1B, 1A) twice, 1B, 9A, (1B, 1A) twice, 1B, 9A, (1B, 1A) 3 times, 1B.
13th row: k.(1B, 1A) into first st., * 7B, (1A, 1B) 3 times, 1A, rep. from * once more, 7B, 1A, 1A, cast on 4 sts.
14th row: p.(1B, 1A) 3 times, * 9B, (1A, 1B) twice, 1A, rep. from * once more, 9B, 1A.
15th row: k.(1A, 1B) into first st., 1A, * 7B, (1A, 1B) 3 times, 1A, rep. from * twice more, cast on 3 sts. [48 sts.]
16th row: p.4B, * (1A, 1B) twice, 1A, 9B, rep. from * twice more, 1A, 1B.
17th row: k.(1B, 1A) into first st., work in patt. to end, ** then across sts. of back and left sleeve to last st., (1A, 1B) into last st. [169(183) sts.]
Working from chart and keeping patt. correct, inc. 1 st. each end of every k. row twice more. [173(187) sts.]
Work 1 row.

Shape Upper Sleeves and Shoulders
Cast off at beg. of next and foll. rows 3 sts. 18 times, 5 sts. 6 times and 7 sts. 10(12) times. [154(168) sts.]
Cast off rem. 19 sts. for neck.

LEFT FRONT

Cast on 46(53) sts. with A.
p. 1 row. k. 1 row. p. 1 row.
Join in B and beg. working patt. from chart, working k. rows from points (A to G) 3 times, then G to C(D) once, and p. rows from point C(D) to A once, then (G to A) twice.
Work 20 rows.
Dec. 1 st. at beg. of next and every 10th row until 43(50) sts. rem.

42

V-neck Casual Sweater

Unisex, V-neck sweater with cable-twist and stocking-stitch panels, set-in sleeves and ribbed welts

★★ Suitable for knitters with some previous experience

MATERIALS

Yarn
Emu Shetland DK
12(12:13:13:14) × 50g. balls

Needles
1 pair 3¼mm.
1 pair 4mm.

MEASUREMENTS

Chest
92(97:102:107:112) cm.
36(38:40:42:44) in.

Length
61(62:63:65:66) cm.
24(24¼:24¾:25½:26) in.

Sleeve Seam
50(51:52:52:53) cm.
19½(20:20½:20½:20¾) in.

TENSION

24 sts. and 30 rows = 10 cm. (4 in.) square over patt. on 4mm. needles. If your tension square does not correspond to these measurements, adjust the needle size used.

ABBREVIATIONS

k.=knit; p.=purl; st(s).=stitch(es); inc.= increase; dec.=decrease; beg.=begin(ning); rem. = remain(ing); rep. = repeat; alt. = alternate; tog. = together; sl. = slip stitch (transfer one stitch from left needle, knitwise unless otherwise stated, to right hand needle.); cont. = continue; patt. = pattern; foll. = following; folls. = follows; mm. = millimetres; cm. = centimetres; in. = inch(es); st.st. = stocking stitch; C3B = cable 3 back: sl. 2 sts. onto cable needle and leave at back of work, k. next st. then p.1, k.1 from cable needle; C3F = cable 3 front: sl. 1 st. onto cable needle and leave at front of work, k. next st., p. the foll. st., then k. the st. on cable needle; p.s.s.o. = pass the sl. st. over.

BACK

Cast on 117(123:129:135:141) sts. with 3¼mm. needles.
1st row: k.1, * p.1, k.1, rep. from * to end.
2nd row: p.1, * k.1, p.1, rep. from * to end.
Rep. 1st and 2nd rows until work measures 9(9:10:10:11) cm. (3½(3½:4:4:4¼) in.), ending with 2nd row.
Change to 4mm. needles and work in patt. as folls.:
1st row: k.16(16:19:19:22), * p.1, C3B, p.1, k.1, p.1, k.6(7:7:8:8), rep. from * to last 10(9:12:11:14) sts., k. to end.
2nd row: p.16(16:19:19:22), * (k.1, p.1) 3 times, k.1, p.6(7:7:8:8), rep. from * to last 10(9:12:11:14) sts., p. to end.
3rd row: k. the k. sts. and p. the p. sts.
4th row: as 2nd row.
5th row: k.16(16:19:19:22), * p.1, k.1, p.1, C3F, p.1, k.6(7:7:8:8), rep. from * to last 10(9:12:11:14) sts. k. to end.
6th row: p.16(16:19:19:22), * (k.1, p.1) 3 times, k.1, p.6(7:7:8:8), rep. from * to last 10(9:12:11:14) sts., p. to end.
7th row: k. the k. sts. and p. the p. sts.
8th row: as 6th row.
Rep. 1st to 8th row throughout.

AT THE SAME TIME, when work measures 39(39:39:40:40) cm. (15¼(15¼:15¼:15¾:15¾) in.) ending with a wrong side row, shape armholes.

Shape Armholes

Cast off 6(6:7:8:9) sts. at beg. of next 2 rows.
Dec. 1 st. at each end of next row and foll. 5(6:7:7:8) alt. rows. [93(97:99:103:105) sts.]
Cont. straight until work measures 20(21: 22:23:24) cm. (7¾(8¼:8½:9:9½) in.) from beg. of armhole shaping, ending with a wrong side row.

Shape Shoulders

Cast off 7(8:8:9:9) sts. at beg. of next 4 rows.
Cast off 8 sts. at beg. of foll. 4 rows.
Cast off rem. 33(33:35:35:37) sts.

FRONT

Work as on back up to 6th row of armhole shapings, ending with a wrong side row. [101(107:111:115:119) sts.]
Cont. as back but AT THE SAME TIME shape neckline.

Shape Neckline

Next row: patt. to centre st. (4th st. on 4th cable), place centre st. unworked on safety pin, turn work and leave rem. sts. on spare needle.
Next row: p.1, sl. 1 purlwise, p.1, p.s.s.o., patt. to end.
Cont. in patt., dec. 1 st. at neck edge (as in previous row) on every alt. row 15(15:16: 16:17) times. [30(32:32:34:34) sts.]
Cont. straight until front reaches same row as back for shoulder shaping.

Shape Shoulder

Work as for back.
Return to sts. on spare needle, and rejoin yarn.
Next row: k.1, sl. 1 knitwise, k.1, p.s.s.o., patt. to end.
Finish to match first side, dec. as just indicated, and reversing all shapings.

SLEEVES

Cast on 57(59:61:63:65) sts. with 3¼mm. needles.
Work in k.1, p.1 rib as on back for 9(9:10:10:11) cm. (3½(3½:4:4:4½) in.), ending with 2nd row.
Change to 4mm. needles.
Next row: k.12(12:13:13:14), * p.1, C3B, p.1, k.1, p.1, k.6(7:7:8:8), rep. from * to last 6(5:6:5:6) sts., k. to end.
Cont. in patt. as set on this row.
AT THE SAME TIME, inc. 1 st. at each end of 3rd row, then inc. 1 st. at each end of every foll. 6th row 18 times, working all incs. in st.st. [95(97:99:101:103) sts.]
Cont. straight until work measures 50(51: 52:52:53) cm. (19½(20:20½:20½:20¾) in.), ending with a wrong side row.

Shape Top

Cast off 6(6:7:8:9) sts. at beg. of next 2 rows.
Dec. 1 st. at each end of every foll. alt. row 26(27:27:27:27) times. [31 sts.]
Dec. 6 sts. at beg. of next 2 rows.
Cast off rem. 19 sts.

NECKBAND

Sew up right shoulder seam.
With 3¼mm. needles and right side facing, pick up 50(50:52:52:54) sts. down left front neck, 1 st. from safety pin (mark with loop of contrasting yarn), 50(50:52: 52:54) sts. up right front neck and 33(33: 35:35:37) sts. from back neck. [134(134: 140:140:146) sts.]
1st row: p.1, * k.1, p.1, rep. from * to 2 sts. before marked st., k.2 sts. tog., p. marked st., k.2 sts. tog., * p.1, k.1, rep. from * to end.
2nd row: p.1, * k.1, p.1, rep. from * to 2 sts. before marked st., sl. 1, p.1, p.s.s.o., k. marked st., k.2 sts. tog., * p.1, k.1, rep. from * to end.
Rep. 1st and 2nd row for 3 cm. (1¼ in.).
Cast off in rib, dec. as usual.

MAKING UP

Press each piece following instructions on ball band.
Sew up left shoulder seam and neckband.
Sew up side and sleeve seams.
Set in sleeves. Press seams if required.

Double-breasted Sand Stitch Jacket 1935

Hip-length, figure-hugging jacket in sand stitch, with cuffed set-in sleeves and patterned collar

★ Suitable for beginners

MATERIALS

Yarn
Sirdar Sportswool
17(17:18) × 50g. balls

Needles
1 pair 4mm.

Buttons
8

MEASUREMENTS

Bust
87(92:97) cm.
34(36:38) in.

Length
59(60:61) cm.
23¼(23½:24) in.

Sleeve seam (with cuff extended)
54 cm.
21¼ in.

TENSION

9 sts. and 13½ rows = 5 cm. (2 in.) square over pattern on 4mm. needles. If your tension square does not correspond to these measurements, adjust the needle size used.

ABBREVIATIONS

k.=knit; p.=purl; st(s).=stitch(es); inc.= increase; dec.=decrease; beg.=begin(ning); rem. = remain(ing); rep. = repeat; alt. = alternate; tog. = together; sl. = slip stitch (transfer one stitch from left needle, knitwise unless otherwise stated, to right hand needle.); cont. = continue; patt. = pattern; foll. = following; folls. = follows; mm. = millimetres; cm. = centimetre(s); in. = inch(es).

BACK

Cast on 103:(109:115) sts. Beg. patt.:
1st row: * k.1, p.1, rep. from * to last st., k.1.
2nd row: k.
These 2 rows form the patt. Proceed until work measures 8 cm. (3¼ in.). Dec. at both ends of next and every foll. 6th row until 93(99:105) sts. rem.
Cont. until work measures 23 cm. (9 in.). Inc. 1 st. at both ends of next and every foll. 8th row until there are 101(107:113) sts. Cont. until work measures 39 cm. (15¼ in.), finishing after a wrong side row.

Shape Armhole
Cast off 3 sts. at beg. of next 2 rows, then dec. 1 st. at both ends of every row until 77(79:81) sts. rem.
Cont. until work measures 19(20:21) cm. (7½(7¾:8¼) in.) from beg. of armholes, after a wrong side row.

Shape Shoulders
Cast off 8 sts. at beg. of next 4 rows and 6(7:8) sts. at beg. of foll. 2 rows. Cast off rem. 33 sts.

LEFT FRONT

Cast on 65(68:71) sts. Work 8 cm. (3¼ in.) in patt. noting that for middle size 1st row will end p.1. Dec. 1 st. at side edge on next and every foll. 6th row until 60(63:66) sts. rem. Cont. until work measures 23 cm. (9 in.). Inc. 1 st. at side edge on next and every foll. 8th row until there are 64(67:70) sts. Cont. until work matches back to armholes, finishing at side edge.

Shape Armhole
Cast off 3 sts. at beg. of next row. Work back. Dec. at side edge on every row until 52(53:54) sts. rem. Cont. until work measures 12(13:14) cm. (4¾(5:5½) in.) from beg. of armhole, finishing at front edge.

Shape Neck
Cast off 27 sts. at beg. of next row, then dec. 1 st. at neck edge on next 3 rows. [22(23:24) sts.]

Cont. until work matches back to outer shoulder.

Shape Shoulder
Cast off 8 sts. at beg. of next 2 side edge rows. Work to side edge.
Cast off rem. 6(7:8) sts.

RIGHT FRONT

Work to correspond with left front, reversing shapings and making 4 pairs of buttonholes, 1st on 1st row of side inc., last just under neck edge, remainder evenly spaced between.
Buttonholes are worked thus, beg. at centre front edge: work 4 sts., cast off 3 sts., (1 st. now on right hand needle), work 14 sts. more, cast off 3 sts., work to end.
Next row: cast on 3 sts. over each group of cast off sts.

SLEEVES

Cast on 45(47:49) sts.
1st row: k.2, * p.1, k.1, rep. from * to last st., k.1.
2nd row: k.1, * p.1, k.1, rep. from * to end. Rep. these 2 rows for 12 cm. (4¾ in.), finishing after a 1st row of rib. Change to patt., beg. with 1st row – (this reverses right side of work). Inc. at both ends of the 7th and every foll. 6th row until there are 75(77:79) sts. Cont. until work measures 54 cm. (21¼ in.), finishing after a wrong side row.

Shape Top
Cast off 3 sts. at beg. of next 2 rows. Dec. 1 st. at both ends of next and every alt. row until 41 sts. rem. Work 1 row. Dec. 1 st. at both ends of every row until 17 sts. rem. Cast off.

COLLAR

Cast on 93 sts. Work 2 rows in k.1 p.1 rib as given for cuffs. Cont. thus:
1st row: k.2, p.2 tog., rib to last 4 sts., p.2 tog., k.2.
2nd row: k.1, p.1, k.2, rib to last 4 sts., k.2, p.1, k.1.
3rd row: k.2, p.2, rib to last 4 sts., p.2, k.2.
4th row: as 2nd.
5th row: as 1st.
6th, 7th and 8th rows: work in rib.
Rep. these 8 rows until 81 sts. rem.
Cast off in rib.

MAKING UP

Sew up side, shoulder and sleeve seams. Set sleeves into armholes. Sew cast off edge of collar to back and sides of neck, to end of dec. sts. (see photograph).
Press seams.
Sew on buttons.

Moss-stitch Woolly Tunic

Long-sleeved, ample tunic in moss stitch throughout, with unshaped armholes, dropped shoulder line, and moss-stitch, shirt-style collar

★ Suitable for beginners

MATERIALS

Yarn

Rowan Classic Tweed DK
12(13) × 50g. balls

Needles

1 pair 3¾mm.
1 pair 4mm.

MEASUREMENTS

Bust

82–87(92–97) cm.
32–34(36–38) in.

Length

69(71) cm.
27(27¾) in.

Sleeve Seam

46(48) cm.
18(18¾) in.

TENSION

21 sts. and 32 rows = 10 cm. (4 in.) square over patt. on 4mm. needles. If your tension square does not correspond to these measurements, adjust the needle size used.

ABBREVIATIONS

k.=knit; p.=purl; st(s).=stitch(es); inc.= increase; dec.=decrease; beg.=begin(ning); rem. = remain(ing); rep. = repeat; alt. = alternate; tog. = together; sl. = slip stitch (transfer one stitch from left needle, knitwise unless otherwise stated, to right hand needle.); cont. = continue; patt. = pattern; foll. = following; folls. = follows; mm. = millimetres; cm. = centimetres; in. = inch(es); st.st. = stocking stitch; m.1 = make one st. purlwise by picking up horizontal loop lying before next st. and working into the back of it.

BACK

Cast on 134(146) sts. with 3¾mm. needles and work in k.1, p.1 rib for 12 cm. (4¾ in.). Change to 4mm. needles and dec. as folls.:
1st size: k.1, * p.2 tog., k.1, p.1, k.2 tog., p.1, k.1, rep. from * to last 5 sts., p.2 tog., k.1, p.1, k.1. 2nd size: k.1, k.1, * p.2 tog., k.1, p.1, k.2 tog., p.1, k.1, rep. from * to last 7 sts., p.2 tog., (k.1, p.1) twice, k.1. [101(111) sts.]

Now work in patt.:
1st row: * k.1, p.1, rep. from * to last st., k.1.
2nd row: as 1st row.
Rep. these 2 rows until work measures 46(50) cm. (18(19½) in.) from cast-on edge.

Shape Armholes

Keeping patt. correct, shape armhole as folls.:
Dec. 1 st. at each end of foll. 10(12) alt. rows. [81(87) sts.]
Now cont. straight in patt. with border as folls.:
1st row: k.9, * p.1, k.1, rep. from * to last 10 sts., p.1, k.9.
2nd row: as 1st row.
Rep. these 2 rows until work measures 18(19) cm. (7(7½) in.) from beg. of armhole shaping.

Shape Neck

Keeping patt. correct, shape neck as folls.:
k.31(34), cast off centre 19 sts., k. to end.
Dec. 1 st. at neck edge on foll. 4 rows. [27(30) sts.]
Cast off. Rejoin yarn to rem. 31(34) sts. and complete to match first side.

FRONT

Work as for back until armhole measures 12(13) cm. (4¾(5¼) in.).

Shape Neck

Keeping patt. and border correct, shape neck as folls.:
k.35(38), cast off centre 11 sts., k. to end.
Dec. 1 st. at neck edge on foll. 4 rows, then dec. 1 st. at neck edge on foll. 4 alt. rows. [27(30) sts.]
Cont. straight for 10 rows.
Cast off.
Rejoin yarn to rem. 35(38) sts. and complete to match first side.

SLEEVES

Cast on 48(50) sts. with 3¾mm. needles and work in k.1, p.1 rib for 12 cm. (4¾ in.).
Change to 4mm. needles.
Inc. row: k.1, (p.1, k.1) 3(4) times, * m.1, k.1, p.1, k.1, rep. from * to last 8 sts., m.1, (k.1, p.1) 4 times. [60(62) sts.]
Work in patt. as for back, inc. 1 st. at each end of every 6th row 13(14) times. [86(90) sts.]
Cont. straight until work measures 46(48) cm. (18(18¾) in.).

Shape Armhole

Dec. 1 st. at each end of foll. 10(12) alt. rows. [66(66) sts.]
Cast off.

COLLAR

Cast on 115(119) sts. with 3¾mm. needles and work collar as folls.:
1st row (right side): k.3, * p.1, k.1, rep. from * to last 4 sts., p.1, k.3.
2nd row: as 1st row.
Rep. 1st and 2nd rows 10 more times.
K. 4 rows.
Cast off.

MAKING UP

Press pieces on wrong side omitting ribbing. Sew up shoulder seams, carefully matching garter st. edges.
Set in sleeve by sewing cast-off edge of sleeve to straight edge of armhole and dec. shaping of sleeve to dec. shaping of body.
Sew up sleeve and side seams, reversing sleeve seam for 6 cm. (2¼ in.) from lower edge for turn back cuff.
Sew collar to neckline: place edges of collar to centre front neck and check that centre back of collar corresponds to centre back neck. Sew seam on right side of back and front, to be hidden when collar is turned down in wear.
Press seams.

Thick Tri-colour Windjammer

Hip-length, very warm sweater, worked in three-coloured pattern, with set-in sleeves and wide, patterned, doubled-over collar

★★★ Suitable for experienced knitters only

MATERIALS

Yarn
Laines Plassard Harmonieuse
5 × 75g. skeins Col. A (Sansas 38)
4 × 75g. skeins Col. B (Tuba 12)
4 × 75g. skeins Col. C (Hautbois 14)

Needles
1 pair 6½mm.

MEASUREMENTS

Bust
82(87:92:97) cm.
32(34:36:38) in.

Length
60(61:61:62) cm.
23½(24:24:24¼) in.

Sleeve Seam
46 cm.
18 in.

TENSION

9 sts. and 15 rows = 10 cm. (4 in.) square over stocking stitch on 6½mm. needles. If your tension square does not correspond to these measurements, adjust the needle size used.

ABBREVIATIONS

k.=knit; p.=purl; st(s).=stitch(es); inc.= increase; dec.=decrease; beg.=begin(ning); rem. = remain(ing); rep. = repeat; alt. = alternate; tog. = together; sl. = slip stitch (transfer one stitch from left needle, knit-wise unless otherwise stated, to right hand needle); cont. = continue; patt. = pattern; foll. = following; folls. = follows; mm. = millimetres; cm. = centimetre(s); in. = inch(es); y.fwd. = yarn forward; y.bk. = yarn back; y.r.n. = yarn round needle: bring yarn over needle from front to back and then under needle; Col. = colour.

BACK

Cast on 38(40:42:44) sts. with A, using thumb method ·
Work one row in k.1, p.1 rib.
Next row: with C, k.1, * y.fwd., sl.1 purl-wise, k.1, rep. from * to last st., k.1.
NB. y.fwd. makes a crossed loop over the sl.st.
Now work in patt. as folls.:
1st row: with B, p.1 * y.bk., sl.1, y.fwd., p.tog. the made st. and the sl.st., rep. from * to last st., p.1.

2nd row: with A, k.1, * y.fwd., sl. the B st., k. the C st., rep. from * to last st., k.1.
3rd row: with C, p.1, * sl. the A st., y.r.n., p. tog. the B and A sts., rep. from * to last st., p.1.
4th row: with B, k.1, * y.fwd., sl. the C st., y.bk., k. tog. the A and C sts., rep. from * to last st., k.1.
5th row: with A, p.1, * sl. the B st., y.r.n., p. the C st., rep. from * to last st., p.1.
6th row: with C, k.1, * y.fwd., sl. the A st., k. tog. the A and B sts., rep. from * to last st., k.1.
These 6 rows form the patt.
Cont. in patt. for another 5 rows.
** Inc. 1 st. each end of next row.
Cont. in patt. for 11 rows, but starting and ending each row with p.2, k.2 alternately.
Inc. 1 st. at each end of next row.
Next row: p.1, y.bk., sl.1, y.fwd., p.1, * y.bk., sl.1, y.fwd., p. tog. the made st. and the sl.st. Rep. from * to last 3 sts., y.bk., sl.l., y.fwd., p.2.
Cont. in patt. for 10 rows.
Inc. 1 st. each end of next row. **
Rep. from ** to ** until there are 46(48:50:52) sts.
Work until back measures 40 cm. (15¾ in.).

Shape Armholes
Cast off 2(2:3:3) sts. at beg. of next 2 rows.
Dec. 1 st. at each end of every alt. row until 36(36:38:38) sts. rem.
Work until armholes measure 18(18:19:20) cm. (7(7:7½:7¾)in.) on the straight.

Shape Shoulders
Cast off 2 sts. at beg. of next 8 rows, then 2(2:3:3) sts. at beg. of foll. 2 rows.
Cast off rem. 16 sts. *loosely*.

FRONT

Work as for back until armholes measure 13(13:14:14) cm. (5(5:5½:5½) in.) on the straight.

Shape Upper Armhole and Neck
Inc. 1 st. each end of next and foll. 4th row.
Work 1 row.
Next row: work 17(17:18:18) sts., cast off 6 sts., work to end. Finish this side first.
1st and alt. rows: patt.
2nd row: cast off 2 sts., patt. to last st., work twice into it.
4th row: cast off 2 sts., patt. to end.
6th row: work 2 tog., work to last st., work twice into last st.
8th row: work 2 tog., work to end.
9th row: work to end.
Rep. 8th and 9th rows once more [12(12:13:13) sts.]

Work 3 rows. Cast off *loosely*.
Join wool to neck edge of rem. sts. and complete in same way.

SLEEVES

Cast on 20(20:22:22) sts. with A.
Work 1 row in k.1, p.1 rib.
Now work in patt. as for back, working rows 1 to 6, and then from ** to **.
Rep. from ** to ** until there are 30(32:34:34) sts.
Work until sleeve measures 46 cm. (18 in.)

Shape Top
Cast off 2(2:3:3) sts. at beg. of next 2 rows.
Dec. 1 st. at each end of every 3rd row until 22 sts. rem., then every 4th row until 16 sts. rem.
Dec. 1 st. each end of next 3 rows.
Cast off *loosely*.

COLLAR

Cast on 54(54:56:56) sts. loosely with A.
Work 16 cm. (6¼ in.) in patt. (rows 1 to 6 inclusive of back).
Cast off *loosely*.

MAKING UP

Sew straight cast off edges of front shoulders to sloped edges of upper back. Set in sleeves, ensuring that shoulder seam slopes slightly to back.
Sew side and sleeve seams.
Join collar to form circle, pin to neck with right side of collar to wrong side of jumper, and collar seam at centre back. Over-sew seam, fold collar in half and slipstitch to seam just made, outside. Take care not to stretch neck, and to sew seam and slip-stitching loosely. DO NOT PRESS.

Soft, Ribbed Ski Sweater

Skinny-rib sweater, just below waist-length, with welts and neckband in alternated rib, and set-in, three-quarter length sleeves

★ Suitable for beginners

MATERIALS

Yarn
Poppleton Eclipse
7(8:8) × 50g. balls

Needles
1 pair 5½mm.
1 pair 6½mm.

MEASUREMENTS

Bust
87(92:97) cm.
34(36:38) in.

Length
49(50:51) cm.
19¼(19½:20) in.

Sleeve Seam
44(45:46) cm.
17¼(17¾:18) in.

TENSION

8 sts. and 10½ rows = 5 cm. (2 in.) square over unpressed rib when slightly stretched widthwise, on 5½mm. needles. If your tension square does not correspond to these measurements, adjust the needle size used.

ABBREVIATIONS

k.=knit; p.=purl; st(s).=stitch(es); inc.= increase; dec.=decrease; beg.=begin(ning); rem. = remain(ing); rep. = repeat; alt. = alternate; tog. = together; sl. = slip stitch (transfer one stitch from left needle, knitwise unless otherwise stated, to right hand needle.); cont. = continue; patt. = pattern; foll. = following; folls. = follows; mm. = millimetres; cm. = centimetre(s); in. = inch(es).

BACK

Cast on 68(72:76) sts. using 4½mm. needles.
1st row: * k.1, p.1, rep. from * to last 2 sts., k.2, rep. this row until work measures 8 cm. (3¼ in.) ending on wrong side and inc. 1 st. at end of last row. [69(73:77) sts.]
Using 5½mm. needles, proceed as folls.:
1st row: k.1, * p.1, k.1, rep. from * to end.
2nd row: k.1, * k.1, p.1, rep. from * to last

2 sts. k.2.
Rep. last 2 rows until work measures 30 cm. (11¾in.) from beg., ending with a 2nd row.

Shape Armhole
Cast off 5(6:7) sts. at beg. of next 2 rows. [59(61:63) sts.] Cont. without further shaping until work measures 48(49:50) cm. (18¾(19¼:19½) in.) from beg. ending with a right side row.

Shape Shoulders
Cast off 3(4:5) sts. at beg. of next 2 rows. Cast off 4 sts. at beg. of foll. 6 rows, ending on right side. [29 sts.]

Shape Neckband
Change to 4½mm. needles. Now alternate rib (i.e. all sts. which would have been k. are p. and vice versa, thus moving rib patt. along 1 st.) as folls.:
1st row (wrong side): k.1, * p.1, k.1, rep. from * to end.
Work 8 rows more in rib.
Cast off very loosely in rib.

FRONT

Work as for back until armhole measures 10 rows less than back to shoulder shaping, ending with a wrong side row. [59(61:63) sts.]

Shape Neck
Rib 21(22:23) sts. and leave on a holder for left side, rib 17 sts. and place on a holder for neckband, rib 21(22:23) sts. for right side.
** Dec. 1 st. at neck edge on next 4 rows then on foll. 2 alt. rows. [15(16:17) sts.]
Work 2 rows.

Shape Shoulder
Cast off 3(4:5) sts. at beg. of next row.
Cast off 4 sts. at beg. of foll. 3 alt. rows.
Break off yarn. **
Rejoin yarn to armhole edge sts. left on a holder for left side, work from ** to **.
Do not break off yarn.

Shape Neckband
Using size 4½mm. needles, pick up and knit, alternating rib as for front neckband, 14 sts. down left side of neck, 17 sts. from holder for neckband, 14 sts. up right side of neck. [45 sts.]
Work 8 more rows in rib.
Cast off loosely in rib.

SLEEVES

Cast on 38(40:42) sts. using 4½mm. needles.
1st row: * k.1, p.1, rep. from * to last 2 sts., k.2. Rep. last row until work measures 4 cm. (1½ in.) ending on wrong side, inc. 1 st. at end of last row. [39(41:43) sts.]
With 5½mm. needles, cont. in rib, alternating rib on first row, and inc. 1 st. at each end of 9th and every foll. 8th row until there are 57(59:61) sts. on the needle. Cont. without further shaping until sleeve measures 44(45:46) cm. (17¼(17¾:18) in.) from beg. ending on wrong side.
Cast off loosely in rib.

MAKING UP

Sew up shoulder seams.
Sew up side and sleeve seams, leaving 6(7:8) rows at top of sleeve open.
Sew cast off edge of sleeve around armhole, sewing last few rows of sleeve to cast off sts. under arm.
Press all seams.

Textured Shawl

Huge, warm shawl with fringed ends, in simple moss-stitch pattern throughout

★ Suitable for beginners

MATERIALS

Yarn
Sunbeam Aran Bainin
18 × 50g. balls

Needles
1 pair 6½mm.

MEASUREMENTS

Length
230 cm.
90 in.

Width
51 cm.
20 in.

TENSION

16 sts. = 10 cm. (4 in.) over patt. on 6½mm. needles. If your tension does not correspond to these measurements, adjust the needle size used.

ABBREVIATIONS

k.=knit; p.=purl; st(s).=stitch(es); inc.= increase; dec.=decrease; beg.=begin(ning); rem. = remain(ing); rep. = repeat; alt. = alternate; tog. = together; sl. = slip stitch (transfer one stitch from left needle, knit-wise unless otherwise stated, to right hand needle.); cont. = continue; patt. = pattern; foll. = following; folls. = follows; mm. = millimetres; cm. = centimetres; in. = inch(es); st.st. = stocking stitch.

STOLE

Cast on 81 sts. with 6½mm. needles.
1st row: k.1, * p.1, k.1, rep. from * to end.
This one row forms the patt.
Work until stole is 230 cm. (90 in.) long.
Cast off in patt., i.e. work each st. in patt. before casting it off.

FRINGE AND MAKING UP

Using 6 strands of yarn 51 cm. (20 in.) long for each tassel (or length required), work a fringe along cast on and cast off edges, working a tassel into every 4th st., using crochet hook to pull yarn through stole. Knot each tassel. Press stole.

Hip-length, Shawl-collared Jacket

Hemmed jacket in stocking stitch with set-in sleeves, large doubled collar with front sections worked as extensions of front bands

★ Suitable for beginners

MATERIALS

Yarn
Hayfield Grampian DK
13(13:14:14:15) × 50g. balls

Needles
1 pair 3¼mm.
1 pair 4mm.

Buttons
6

MEASUREMENTS

Bust
82(87:92:97:102) cm.
32(34:36:38:40) in.

Length
55(56:57:58:59) cm.
21½(22:22¼:22¾:23¼) in.

Sleeve Seam
43(44:45:46:47) cm.
16¾(17¼:17¾:18:18½) in.

TENSION

22 sts. and 30 rows = 10 cm. (4 in.) square over stocking stitch on 4mm needles. If your tension square does not correspond to these measurements, adjust the needle size used.

ABBREVIATIONS

k.=knit; p.=purl; st(s).=stitch(es); inc.= increase; dec.=decrease; beg.=begin(ning); rem. = remain(ing); rep. = repeat; alt. = alternate; tog. = together; sl. = slip stitch (transfer one stitch from left needle, knit-wise unless otherwise stated, to right hand needle.); cont. = continue; patt. = pattern; foll. = following; folls. = follows; mm. = millimetres; cm. = centimetre(s); in. = inch(es); p.s.s.o. = pass slipped stitch over; reqd. = required; st.st. = stocking stitch.

BACK

Cast on 97(103:109:115:121) sts. with 3¼mm needles.
Beg. with a k. row, work 9 rows in st.st. then k.1 row to mark hemline.
Change to 4mm. needles and beg. with a k. row, cont. in st.st. until work measures 37cm. (14½ in.) from hemline, ending with a p. row. **

Shape Armholes
Cast off 5(5:6:6:7) sts. at beg. of next 2 rows.
Next row: k.1, sl.1, k.1, p.s.s.o., k. to last 3 sts., k.2 tog., k.1.
Next row: p. to end.
Rep. the last 2 rows 3(4:4:5:5) times more. [79(83:87:91:95) sts.]
Cont. without shaping until armholes measure 18(19:20:21:22) cm., 7(7½:7¾: 8¼:8½) in.), ending with a p. row.

Shape Shoulders
Cast off 5(5:6:6:7) sts. at beg. of next 6 rows, then 5(6:5:6:5) sts. at beg. of next 2 rows. [39(41:41:43:43) sts.]

COLLAR

Cont. on these sts., work 14 rows.
Next row: k.2, m. 1 by picking up loop bet-ween sts. and k. into the back of it, k. to last 2 sts., m. 1, k.2.
Work 5 rows.
Rep. the last 6 rows 6 times more, then the first row again. [55(57:57:59:59) sts.] .
Work 17 rows.
Next row: k.2, k.2 tog., k. to last 4 sts., sl.1, k.1, p.s.s.o., k.2.
Work 5 rows.
Rep. the last 6 rows 6 times more, then the first row again. [39(41:41:43:43) sts.]
Work 13 rows. Cast off.

LEFT FRONT

Cast on 47(50:53:56:59) sts. with 3¼mm. needles and work as for back to **.

Shape Armhole
Cast off 5(5:6:6:7) sts. at beg. of next row.
Next row: p. to end.
Next row: k.1, sl.1, k.1, p.s.s.o., k. to end.
Rep. the last 2 rows 3(4:4:5:5) times more. [38(40:42:44:46) sts.]
Cont. without shaping until armhole measures the same as back, ending with a p. row.

Shape Shoulder
Cast off 5(5:6:6:7) sts. at beg. of next row and foll. 2 alt. rows, then 5(6:5:6:5) sts. at beg. of foll. alt. row.
Cast off rem. 18(19:19:20:20) sts.

RIGHT FRONT

Work to match left front, reversing all shapings.

SLEEVES

Cast on 53(55:57:59:61) sts. with 3¼mm. needles.
1st row: k.1, * p.1, k.1, rep. from * to end.
2nd row: p.1, * k.1, p.1, rep. from * to end.
Rep. these 2 rows for 10 cm. (4 in.), ending with a 1st row.
Next row: rib 3(4:5:6:7), * m. 1, rib 12, rep. from * 3 times more, m. 1, rib to end. [58(60:62:64:66) sts.]
Change to 4mm. needles and beg. with a k. row cont. in st.st., m. 1 st. at each end of 5th and every foll. 10th(10th: 8th:8th:8th) row until there are 76(80:84:88:92) sts., then cont. without shaping until sleeve seam measures 43(44: 45:46:47) cm. 16¾(17¼:17¾:18:18½) in., ending with a p. row.

Shape Top
Cast off 5(5:6:6:7) sts. at beg. of next 2 rows.

Dec. as on back armholes at each end of next and every alt. row until 40(42:44:46:48) sts. rem., ending with a p. row.

Cast off 2 sts. at beg. of next 6(6:6:8:8) rows, then 3 sts. at beg. of next 4 rows.

Cast off rem. 16(18:20:18:20) sts.

LEFT FRONT BAND AND COLLAR

Cast on 27 sts. with 4mm. needles and work in st.st. for 37 cm. (14½ in.) (same length as back and fronts from hemline to armholes), ending with a p. row.

Next row: k.10, m. 1, k.7, m. 1, k.10.

Next row: p. to end.

Next row: k.11, m. 1, k.7, m. 1, k.11.

Cont. to inc. at each side of 7 centre sts. on every alt. row until there are 79 sts., then cont. without shaping until straight edge of collar measures the same as front edge to shoulder, ending with a p. row.

Cast off.

Mark position of buttons with pins as folls.:

1st pin on 5th row from beg., 2nd pin level with first row of shaping, then 4 more at equal distances between these two.

RIGHT FRONT BAND AND COLLAR

Work as given for left front band and collar, making buttonholes to correspond with position of pins as folls.:

(right side facing) k.5, cast off 3, k. to last 8 sts., cast off 3, k.5.

On next row cast on 3 sts. over each 3 cast off.

MAKING UP

Press work according to instructions on ball band.

Join shoulder seams leaving 18(19: 19:20:20) sts. at front edge free.

Sew in sleeves.

Join side and sleeve seams. Turn up hem at lower edge and slipstitch.

Sew on front bands. Sew top edge of collar and top part of front to edges of back collar. Fold front bands and collar in half to inside and slipstitch. Sew round double buttonholes. Press seams. Sew on buttons.

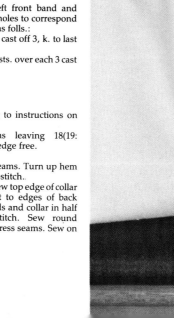

Striped, V-neck Mohair Sweater

Simple sweater in stocking stitch with three coloured mohair stripe pattern, drop shoulders, ribbed welts and neck band

★ Suitable for beginners

MATERIALS

Yarn
Lister-Lee Mohair
9(10:11) × 25g. balls Col. A (Green)
3(3:4) × 25g. balls Col. B (Grey)
1(1:1) × 25g. balls Col. C (White)

Needles
1 pair 5mm.
1 pair 6½mm.

MEASUREMENTS

Bust
87(92:97) cm.
34(36:38) in.

Length from Shoulder
66(67:68) cm.
26(26¼:26¾) in.

Sleeve Seam
46 cm.
18 in.

TENSION

13 sts. and 18 rows = 10 cm. (4 in.) square over stocking stitch on 6½mm. needles. If your tension square does not correspond to these measurements, adjust the needle size used.

ABBREVIATIONS

k.=knit; p.=purl; st(s).=stitch(es); inc.= increase; dec.=decrease; beg.=begin(ning); rem. = remain(ing); rep. = repeat; alt. = alternate; tog. = together; sl. = slip stitch (transfer one stitch from left needle, knit-wise unless otherwise stated, to right hand needle.); cont. = continue; patt. = pattern; foll. = following; folls. = follows; mm. = millimetres; cm. = centimetre(s); in. = inch(es); A = colour A (green); B = colour B (grey); C = colour C (white); k.2 tog. b. = knit 2 together through back; st.st. = stocking stitch.

BACK

Cast on 54(56:60) sts. with 5mm. needles using A.
Work in k.1, p.1, rib for 12 cm. (4¾ in.).
Next row: k.5(6:8) sts. inc. in next st.,

* k.5., inc. 1 st. in next st., rep. from * 6 times more, k.6(7:9) sts. [62(64:68) sts.]
Change to 6½mm. needles and cont. in st.st. until work measures 20 cm. (7¾ in.) from cast on edge.
** Change to B, work 5 cm. (2 in.). Change to C, work 2 rows. Rep. from ** twice more. Cont. in A only until work measures 46 cm. (18 in.) from cast on edge. Mark each end of last row with waste yarn (armhole markers).

*** Cont. in st.st. for a further 20(21:22) cm. (7¾(8¼:8½) in.) from markers.
Next row: cast off 20(20:21) sts., k.22(24:26) sts., cast off rem. sts. Slip centre back sts. onto a spare needle.

FRONT

Work as back to ***.

Divide for Neck
Next row: k.31(32:34) sts., leave these sts. on a spare needle for left front, k. to end on rem. 31(32:34) sts.

Work in st.st. for 3 rows ending at neck edge.

Shape Neck
1st row: k.1, k.2 tog., k. to end.
2nd row: p.
3rd row: k.
4th row: p. to last 3 sts., p.2 tog., p.1.
Cont. to dec. 1 st. at neck edge on every foll. 3rd row until 20(21:22) sts. rem.
Cont. straight until work measures the same as back from markers (ending with a p. row). Cast off.
Rejoin yarn at front neck, work to match right front reversing all shapings.

SLEEVES

Cast on 30(32:34) sts. with 5mm. needles using A, and work in k.1, p.1 rib for 10 cm. (4 in.).
Next row: k.1(2:3) sts., inc. 1 st. in next st., * k.2., inc. 1 st. in next st., rep. from * 8 times more, k.1(2:3). [40(42:44) sts.].
Change to 6½mm. needles, cont. in st.st.
Change to B, work 5 cm. (2 in.) *at the same time* inc. 1 st. at each end of the 5th and every foll. 7th row until there are 58(60:62) sts.
Change to C, work 2 rows. Change to B, work 5 cm. (2 in.).
Change to C, work 2 rows.
Cont. in A only until work measures 46 cm. (18 in.) from cast on edge (or required length). Cast off.

NECKBAND

Sew up right shoulder seam.
With right side facing and 5mm. needles using B, pick up and k. 31(33:35) sts. down left front, 31(33:35) sts. up right front neck, then k. across sts. left on spare needle of centre back.
Next row: rib to within 2 sts. of centre front, p.2., rib to end.
Next row: rib to within 2 sts. of centre front, k.2 tog., k.2 tog. b., rib to end.
Rep. last two rows twice more. Cast off in rib.

MAKING UP

Sew up left shoulder seam. Sew up side seams to markers.
Sew up sleeve seams, then sew cast off edge to armhole edge. Do not press. For a luxurious effect lightly brush mohair.

Turtle-necked Sloppy Joe

Two-tone, hip-length loose sweater, with contrast welts in difficult twisted pattern, body and turtle neck in fisherman's rib

★★★ This pattern is suitable for *very* experienced knitters only

MATERIALS

Yarn

Jaeger Luxury Spun 4 ply
10(11:11:12:12) × 50g. balls (Main Colour)
3(3:3:3:3) × 50g. balls (Contrast Colour)

Needles

1 pair 2¾mm.
1 pair 3mm.

MEASUREMENTS

Bust

82(87:92:97:102) cm.
32(34:36:38:40) in.

Length (from top of shoulders)

58(60:61:61) cm.
22¾(23½:23½:24:24) in.

Sleeve seam

44 cm.
17¼ in.

TENSION

15 sts. and 30 rows = 5 cm. (2 in.) square over Fisherman's Rib on 3mm. needles. If your tension square does not correspond to these measurements, adjust the needle size used.

ABBREVIATIONS

k.=knit; p.=purl; st(s).=stitch(es); inc.=increase; dec.=decrease; beg.=begin(ning); rem. = remain(ing); rep. = repeat; alt. = alternate; tog. = together; sl. = slip stitch (transfer one stitch from left needle, knitwise unless otherwise stated, to right hand needle.); cont. = continue; patt. = pattern; foll. = following; folls. = follows; mm. = millimetres; cm. = centimetre(s); in. = inch(es); tw.2 R. = k. into front of 2nd st. on left needle then k. into front of 1st. st. and slip both sts. off needle together; tw.2 L. = k. into back of 2nd st. on left needle then k. into the front of the 1st st. and slip both sts. off needle together; k.1 D. = k. next st. but through the loop of the row below; M = main colour; C = contrast colour.

BACK

Cast on 142(150:158:166:174) sts. with 2¾mm. needles and C.
1st row (right side): k.1, * tw.2 R., rep. from * to last st., k.1.
2nd row: p.
3rd row: k.1, * tw.2 L., rep. from * to last st., k.1.
4th row: p.

The last 4 rows form border patt. Rep. them until work measures 20 cm. (7¾ in.) at centre from start, ending with 1st row and dec. 1 st. at end of last row. [141(149:157:165:173) sts.] Break C.
Join in M, change to 3mm. needles and fisherman's rib patt. as folls.:
1st row: p.1, * k.1 D., p.1, rep. from * to end.
2nd row (right side): k.1, * p.1, k.1, rep. from * to end.
These 2 rows form fisherman's rib patt.
Work straight in patt. until back measures 47 cm. (18½ in.) at centre from start, ending with right side facing.

Shape Armholes

Cast off 5 sts. at beg. of next 2 rows, then dec. 1 st. at each end of next and every foll. 3rd row until 111(115:119:123:127) sts. rem., then on every foll. 4th row until 105(109:113:117:121) sts. rem. **
Work straight until back measures 66(67:67:69:69) cm. (26(26¼:26¼:27:27) in.) at centre from start, ending with right side facing.

Shape Shoulders

Cast off 3 sts. at beg. of next 4(6:8:10:12) rows, then 2 sts. at beg. of next 20(18:16:14:12) rows. Cast off rem. 53(55:57:59:61) sts.

FRONT

Work as for back from ** to **.
Work straight until front measures 63(65:65:66:66) cm. (24¾(25½:25½:26:26) in.) at centre from start, ending with right side facing.
Here divide for neck.
Next row: patt. 44(45:46:47:48), turn and leave rem. sts. on a spare needle.
Cont. on these 44(45:46:47:48) sts. for first side and work 1 row straight.
Dec. 1 st. at neck edge on next and every foll. alt. row until 37(38:39:40:41) sts. rem.
Work 1 row straight.
Cont. dec. 1 st. at neck edge on alt. rows as before and at the same time shape shoulder by casting off 3 sts. at beg. of next and foll. 1(2:3:4:5) alt. rows, then 2 sts. at beg. of foll. 9(8:7:6:5) alt. rows.
Now keep neck edge straight and cont. shaping shoulder by casting off 2 sts. at beg. of alt. row.
With right side facing, rejoin yarn to rem. sts., cast off centre 17(19:24:23:25) sts., patt. to end.
Finish to correspond with first side.

SLEEVES

Cast on 74(76:76:80:80) sts. with 2¾mm. needles and C., and work 15 cm. (5¾ in.) in

border patt., ending with 1st row, and inc. 1 st. at end of last row. [75(77:77:81:81) sts.] Break C.
Join in M, change to 3mm. needles.
Starting with 1st row, work in fisherman's rib patt., shaping sides by inc. 1 st. at each end of 15th(13th:13th:17th:17th) and every foll. 16th(14th:14th:12th:12th) row until there are 97(103:103:109:109) sts., taking inc. sts. into rib.
Work straight until sleeve seam measures 52 cm. (20½ in.), ending with right side facing.

Shape Top

Cast off 5 sts. at beg. of next 2 rows, then dec. 1 st. at each end of next and every foll. 4th row until 69(75:75:81:81) sts. rem.
Work 3 rows straight, then dec. 1 st. at each end of next and every alt. row until 55 sts. rem.
Work 1 row straight, then dec. 1 st. at each end of every row until 35 sts. rem.
Cast off 3 sts. at beg. of next 4 rows. Cast off rem. 23 sts.

COLLAR

Cast on 155(159:163:167:171) sts. with 3mm. needles and M.
1st row: k.1, * p.1, k.1, rep. from * to end.
2nd row: p.1, * k.1, p.1, rep. from * to end.
Rep. last 2 rows 3 times more, then 1st row again.
Change to fisherman's rib, starting with 1st row and work straight until collar measures 17 cm. (6½ in.) at centre from start, ending with 1st row.
Cast off loosely in rib.

MAKING UP

Press work lightly on wrong side, taking care not to spoil the patt.
Sew up shoulder, side and sleeve seams, insert sleeves. Fold welt and cuffs to wrong side and slipstitch lightly in position on wrong side.
Sew up short ends of collar, then pin cast on edge of collar in position round neck with seam at centre back, easing in any fullness.
Press all seams.

Raised Leaf-pattern Top

Allover leaf-design top, with three-quarter length set-in sleeves, ribbed welts and round neckline

★★ Suitable for knitters with some previous experience

MATERIALS

Yarn
Sirdar Countrystyle DK
10(10) × 50g. balls

Needles
1 pair 3¼mm.
1 pair 4(4½)mm.
2 stitch holders

MEASUREMENTS

Bust
92(97) cm.
36(38) in.

Length
58(59) cm.
22¾(23¼) in.

Sleeve Seam
28 cm.
11 in.

TENSION

13 sts. and 15 rows (12 sts. and 14 rows) = 5 cm. (2 in.) square over patt. on 4(4½)mm. needles. If your tension square does not correspond to these measurements, adjust the needle size used.

ABBREVIATIONS

k.=knit; p.=purl; st(s).=stitch(es); inc.= increase; dec.=decrease; beg.=begin(ning); rem. = remain(ing); rep. = repeat; alt. = alternate; tog. = together; sl. = slip stitch (transfer one stitch from left needle, knit-wise unless otherwise stated, to right hand needle.); cont. = continue; patt. = pattern; foll. = following; folls. = follows; mm. = millimetres; cm. = centimetres; in. = inch(es); st.st. = stocking stitch; y.o. = yarn over, to make 1 st.; p.s.s.o. = pass the slipped st. over; p.u. = pick up the loop before next st. and k. or p. into the back of it.
N.B. The 2nd size is worked over the same number of sts. as the 1st size, but using larger needles.

BACK

Cast on 121 sts. with 3¼mm. needles.
Work in k.1, p.1 rib for 5 cm. (2 in.), inc. in last row as folls.:
(Rib 11, p.u.) 10 times, rib 11. [131 sts.]
Change to 4(4½)mm. needles and work as folls.:
1st row: k.3, * y.o., p.3, sl.1, k.1, p.s.s.o., k.3, k.2 tog., p.3, y.o., k.1, rep. from * to last 2 sts., k.2.
2nd row: p.4, * k.3, p.5, k.3, p.3, rep. from * to last st., p.1.
3rd row: k.3, * y.o., k.1, p.3, sl.1, k.1, p.s.s.o., k.1, k.2 tog., p.3, k.1, y.o., k.1, rep. from * to last 2 sts., k.2.
4th row: p.5, * k.3, p.3, k.3, p.5, rep. from * to end.
5th row: k.3, * y.o., k.2, p.3, sl.1, k.2 tog., p.s.s.o., p.3, k.2, y.o., k.1, rep. from * to last 2 sts., k.2.
6th row: p.6, * k.3, p.1, k.3, p.7, rep. from * to end, ending last rep. p.6.
7th row: k.6, * p.7, k.7, rep. from * to end, ending last rep. k.6.
8th row: p.6, * k.7, p.7, rep. from * to end, ending last rep. p.6.
9th row: k.3, * k.1, k.2 tog., p.3, y.o., k.1, y.o., p.3, sl.1, k.1, p.s.s.o., k.2, rep. from * to last 2 sts., k.2.
10th row: as 4th row.
11th row: k.3, * k.2 tog., p.3, k.1, y.o., k.1, y.o., k.1, p.3, sl.1, k.1, p.s.s.o., k.1, rep. from * to last 2 sts., k.2.
12th row: as 2nd row.
13th row: k.2, k.2 tog., * p.3, k.2, y.o., k.1., y.o., k.2, p.3, sl.1, k.2 tog., p.s.s.o., rep. from * to end, ending last rep. sl.1, k.1, p.s.s.o., k.2.
14th row: p.3, * k.3, p.7, k.3, p.1, rep. from * to last 2 sts., p.2.
15th row: as 8th row.
16th row: as 7th row.
Rep. these 16 patt. rows throughout.
Work straight until back measures 38 cm. (15 in.) from beg.
Place a marker at both ends of work.
Work straight until back measures 56(57) cm. (22(22¼) in.) from beg.

Shape Neck
* Patt. 48 sts., turn. Leave rem. sts. on a holder.
Dec. 1 st. at neck edge on next row.

Work 1 row.
Cast off 2 sts. at beg. of next row.
Dec. 1 st. at neck edge on next and foll. alt. rows until 43 sts. rem.*
Work straight until 8 rows have been completed from beg. of neck shaping.
Cast off.
Return to rem. sts.
With right side facing, sl. the next 35 sts. onto a holder.
Rejoin yarn and patt. to end of row.
Dec. 1 st. at neck edge on next row.
Cast off 2 sts. at neck edge on next row.
Dec. 1 st. at neck edge on foll. 2 alt. rows.
Work 1 row. Cast off.

FRONT

Work as for back until 16 rows less than back have been worked.

Shape Neck

Work as for back from * to *.
Work straight until same length as back.
Cast off.
Return to rem. sts.
Sl. the next 35 sts. onto a holder, then complete to match first side, reversing all shapings.

SLEEVES

Cast on 59 sts. with 3¼mm. needles.
Work in k.1, p.1 rib for 10 rows, inc. on last row as folls.:

Rib 1, p.u., (rib 2, p.u.,) 28 times, rib 1, p.u., rib 1. [89 sts.]
Change to 4(4½)mm. needles and work in patt. as given for back.
Work straight until 64(60) rows of patt. have been worked.

Shape Top

Inc. 1 st. at both ends of the next and every foll. alt. row until there are 105 sts., working the extra sts. at both ends in st.st.
Cast off.

NECKBAND

Sew up left shoulder seam.
With right side facing and 3¼mm. needles, pick up and k.11 sts. from right side back neck, k. across 35 sts. at centre back neck, pick up and k.11 sts. from left side back neck and 17 sts. from left side front neck, k. across 35 sts. from centre front neck, and pick up and k.17 sts. from right side front neck.
Work in k.1, p.1 rib for 5 cm. (2 in.).
Cast off fairly loosely in rib.

MAKING UP

Press work on wrong side under a damp cloth.
Sew up right shoulder and neckband seam.
Fold neckband in half onto wrong side, and sew down.
Sew sleeves into armholes between markers.
Sew up side and sleeve seams.